THE WAY PEOPLE LIVE

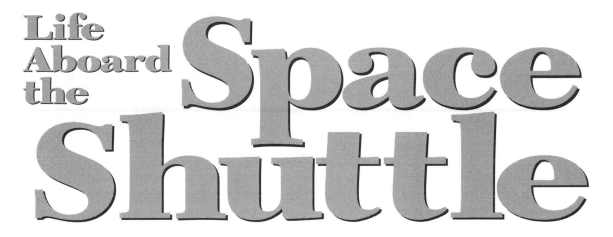

Life Aboard the Space Shuttle

Titles in The Way People Live series include:

The Way People Live

Life Aboard the Space Shuttle

by
Robert Taylor

LUCENT BOOKS
SAN DIEGO, CALIFORNIA

THOMSON
GALE

Detroit • New York • San Diego • San Francisco
Boston • New Haven, Conn. • Waterville, Maine
London • Munich

Library of Congress Cataloging-in-Publication Data

Taylor, Robert, 1948–
    Life aboard the space shuttle / by Robert Taylor.
        p. cm. — (The way people live)
Includes bibliographical references and index.
Summary: Discusses the early years of travel in space shuttles, including the
construction of the first shuttles and the training of the crews.
    ISBN 1-59018-154-9   (hardback : alk. paper)
    1. Space shuttles—Juvenile literature.   2. Manned space flight—Juvenile liter-
ature.   [1. Space shuttles.   2. Manned space flight.   3. Outer space—
Exploration.   4. Astronauts.]   I. Title. II. Series.
    TL795.515   .T3897   2002
    629.44'1—dc21

2001006125

Contents

Discovering the Humanity in Us All

Books in The Way People Live series focus on groups of people in a wide variety of circumstances, settings, and time periods. Some books focus on different cultural groups, others, on people in a particular historical time period, while others cover people involved in a specific event. Each book emphasizes the daily routines, personal and historical struggles, and achievements of people from all walks of life.

To really understand any culture, it is necessary to strip the mind of the common notions we hold about groups of people. These stereotypes are the archenemies of learning. It does not even matter whether the stereotypes are positive or negative; they are confining and tight. Removing them is a challenge that's not easily met, as anyone who has ever tried it will admit. Ideas that do not fit into the templates we create are unwelcome visitors—ones we would prefer remain quietly in a corner or forgotten room.

The cowboy of the Old West is a good example of such confining roles. The cowboy was courageous, yet soft-spoken. His time (it is always a he, in our template) was spent alternatively saving a rancher's daughter from certain death on a runaway stagecoach, or shooting it out with rustlers. At times, of course, he was likely to get a little crazy in town after a trail drive, but for the most part, he was the epitome of inner strength. It is disconcerting to find out that the cowboy is human, even a bit childish. Can it really be true that cowboys would line up to help the cook on the trail drive grind coffee, just hoping he would give them a little stick of peppermint candy that came with the coffee shipment? The idea of tough cowboys vying with one another to help "Coosie" (as they called their cooks) for a bit of candy seems silly and out of place.

So is the vision of Eskimos playing video games and watching MTV, living in prefab housing in the Arctic. It just does not fit with what "Eskimo" means. We are far more comfortable with snow igloos and whale blubber, harpoons and kayaks.

Although the cultures dealt with in Lucent's The Way People Live series are often historically and socially well known, the emphasis is on the personal aspects of life. Groups of people, while unquestionably affected by their politics and their governmental structures, are more than those institutions. How do people in a particular time and place educate their children? What do they eat? And how do they build their houses? What kinds of work do they do? What kinds of games do they enjoy? The answers to these questions bring these cultures to life. People's lives are revealed in the particulars and only by knowing the particulars can we understand these cultures' will to survive and their moments of weakness and greatness.

This is not to say that understanding politics does not help to understand a culture. There is no question that the Warsaw ghetto, for example, was a culture that was brought about by the politics and social ideas of Adolf

Hitler and the Third Reich. But the Jews who were crowded together in the ghetto cannot be understood by the Reich's politics. Their life was a day-to-day battle for existence, and the creativity and methods they used to prolong their lives is a vital story of human perseverance that would be denied by focusing only on the institutions of Hitler's Germany. Knowing that children as young as five or six outwitted Nazi guards on a daily basis, that Jewish policemen helped the Germans control the ghetto, that children attended secret schools in the ghetto and even earned diplomas—these are the things that reveal the fabric of life, that can inspire, intrigue, and amaze.

Books in The Way People Live series allow both the casual reader and the student to see humans as victims, heroes, and onlookers. And although humans act in ways that can fill us with feelings of sorrow and revulsion, it is important to remember that "hero," "predator," and "victim" are dangerous terms. Heaping undue pity or praise on people reduces them to objects, and strips them of their humanity.

Seeing the Jews of Warsaw only as victims is to deny their humanity. Seeing them only as they appear in surviving photos, staring at the camera with infinite sadness, is limiting, both to them and to those who want to understand them. To an object of pity, the only appropriate response becomes "Those poor creatures!" and that reduces both the quality of their struggle and the depth of their despair. No one is served by such two-dimensional views of people and their cultures.

With this in mind, The Way People Live series strives to flesh out the traditional, two-dimensional views of people in various cultures and historical circumstances. Using a wide variety of primary quotations—the words not only of the politicians and government leaders, but of the real people whose lives are being examined—each book in the series attempts to show an honest and complete picture of a culture removed from our own by time or space.

By examining cultures in this way, the reader will notice not only the glaring differences from his or her own culture, but also will be struck by the similarities. For indeed, people share common needs—warmth, good company, stability, and affirmation from others. Ultimately, seeing how people really live, or have lived, can only enrich our understanding of ourselves.

The Problems of Life in Space and How the Shuttle Solves Them

Human beings cannot live in space. Millions of years of evolution have equipped people to survive only in conditions as they exist on, or very near, Earth's surface. Humans depend on an environment that contains oxygen to breathe, air pressure to keep the body from either collapsing or exploding, water to drink, food to eat, and protection from extreme heat and cold. People also need to be shielded from harmful radiation generated by the sun, and Earth's atmosphere provides that protection.

The hospitable environment on Earth is quite the opposite of the lethal conditions found in space. Beyond Earth's atmosphere, there is no life-sustaining oxygen to breathe. In the absence of air pressure, gas bubbles would form in the blood, causing it to boil. The skin would swell and internal organs would rupture. Without the protection of Earth's atmosphere, the surface of the body exposed to the rays of the sun would quickly soar to 250 degrees Fahrenheit; the temperature of the surface shielded from the sun would plunge to minus 250 degrees Fahrenheit. No human could withstand the torment for more than thirty seconds before dying.

In order to live in an environment as hostile as space, humans must re-create the conditions that sustain life on Earth. That is what spacecraft like the space shuttle do. They are biospheres, artificial Earthlike habitats, that use engineering to replicate basic features of nature.

Evolution of Spacecraft Habitats

Early space vehicles barely met the standards required for mere survival. The astronauts these vessels carried aloft had to withstand forces more than ten times greater than gravity on liftoff. They were compelled to spend their time in space strapped into their seats, wearing cumbersome pressurized suits and helmets. They had to breathe pure oxygen. Their food consisted of tasteless paste squeezed out of tubes, and when they had to urinate or defecate, they did so into adult diapers or sealable bags that rarely worked adequately. To be an astronaut in those taxing circumstances required the strength, stamina, and mental toughness of a military test pilot.

The space shuttle—designed and built between 1969 and 1982 by the U.S. National Aeronautics and Space Administration (NASA) —represents an impressive leap beyond those first space vehicles. Shuttle astronauts are required to wear pressure suits and stay in their seats only during launch and landing. The rest of the time, they can move freely about the cabin wearing only shorts and T-shirts. The composition and pressure of the air in the cabin is almost exactly that on Earth, so the space travelers don't need special equipment to breathe. They can heat their food in an oven and eliminate body wastes in a toilet. Cabin temperature is maintained at normal levels and the maximum g forces they have to en-

Large clouds of smoke billow as the space shuttle blasts off.

dure are less than those experienced on many amusement park roller coasters.

Shuttle Layout

The space shuttle is intricately designed to protect the astronauts who fly on it from the hostility of the space environment and the rigors of both liftoff and landing. By mid-2001, when the spacecraft made its hundredth flight, more than four hundred astronauts had lived and worked on it in conditions that more closely replicate those on Earth than any other vessel in the history of space exploration.

The shuttle consists of three components: the orbiter, where the crew live and work; a liquid-fuel tank; and two identical solid-fuel rocket boosters, which provide more than 6 million pounds of thrust on liftoff. Unlike previous spacecraft, which were built for one flight only, the shuttle is reusable. Each of the four orbiters that comprise the shuttle fleet is designed to make a hundred trips. The shuttle is also versatile: it launches satellites into space, services them while they are in orbit, and returns them to Earth for major overhauls; it is a laboratory where the astronauts can perform scientific experiments; and it is also an orbiting construction platform capable of feats as complicated as building the International Space Station.

The orbiter is the heart of the space shuttle system, providing a home in space for the crew. It is about the size of a DC-9 jet airliner: 122 feet long and 57 feet high, with a wingspan of 78 feet. Empty, it weighs 165,000 pounds, and it can carry a cargo, or payload, of up to 65,000 pounds. It can support a crew of seven astronauts for sixteen days.

The orbiter's hull is constructed of aluminum and titanium, both strong yet lightweight metals. It is divided into three sections. The forward fuselage houses the crew compartment, the landing gear, and the reaction control engines, which help the vehicle to maneuver in space. The mid-fuselage houses the cargo bay, a large area with two massive doors where the mission payloads are stored; the fuel cells, which provide electricity while the shuttle is in orbit; hydrogen and oxygen tanks to power the fuel cells; and oxygen and nitrogen tanks to maintain the atmosphere of the crew compartment. The aft fuselage encompasses the three main engines, used only during the launch, and the orbital maneuvering system, which, along with the reaction control engines, alters the course and altitude of the shuttle while in orbit.

Life Support

The life-support system maintains an atmosphere in the crew cabin that is almost identical to that at sea level on Earth: 80 percent nitrogen and 20 percent oxygen at a pressure of 14.2 pounds per square inch. It also filters out the toxic carbon dioxide that the astronauts produce when they exhale.

The thermal protection system and the cargo bay doors keep the temperature of the crew compartment within an acceptable range. The thermal protection system consists of quilted insulation blankets affixed to the craft's skin onto which are glued thirty-two thousand hand-installed heat-resistant tiles. Together the quilts and tiles protect the crew from the minus 250 degrees Fahrenheit cold of space to the plus 3,000 degrees caused by the friction of Earth's atmosphere on reentry. The cargo bay doors remain open all the time the shuttle is in orbit. Their interior surfaces contain radiators that dissipate heat built up in the cabin from the astronauts' bodies and the orbiter's electronics.

Water for drinking and bathing is not carried from Earth—water is extremely heavy and would add an unacceptable amount of weight. Rather, it is produced while the shuttle is in orbit by the fuel cells, which combine oxygen and hydrogen to generate electricity and give off pure water as a by-product.

On Earth humans are protected from harmful radiation by the atmosphere. The orbiter's metallic skin and thermal protection system are thick enough to block ultraviolet rays, but gamma rays and X rays are so highly energized, they overpower the electromagnetic bonds that hold together the atoms of these protective layers and penetrate the crew compartment. The space shuttle circumvents the worst of this potentially deadly radiation by

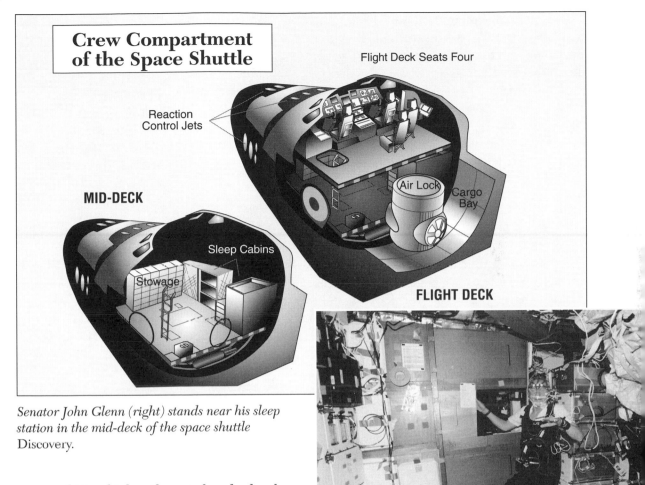

Crew Compartment of the Space Shuttle

Flight Deck Seats Four

Reaction Control Jets

MID-DECK

Sleep Cabins

Stowage

Air Lock

Cargo Bay

FLIGHT DECK

Senator John Glenn (right) stands near his sleep station in the mid-deck of the space shuttle Discovery.

never orbiting higher than six hundred miles (usually it orbits at an altitude of about two hundred miles), thus remaining within Earth's protective magnetic shield, which deflects much of the radiation back into space. This keeps the astronauts inside the shuttle quite safe. When a mission calls for venturing outside the spacecraft, the space walks are timed to avoid periods of peak solar radiation emission.

The Crew Compartment

The crew compartment is an airtight chamber with three levels, or decks. The flight deck is the topmost. It's where the commander and pilot sit to operate the shuttle. It contains the flight controls—some two thousand knobs, switches, and displays—and an aft workstation where astronauts can carry out assignments. Below the flight deck is the mid-deck, where there are accommodations for eating, sleeping, and personal hygiene, as well as storage lockers for gear and experiments. The bottom level is an equipment bay, which has room for garbage, some of the life-support equipment, and additional stowage.

The compartment has twelve windows that allow the astronauts to look down at Earth and into the payload bay. At the back of the mid-deck, there is an air lock that space-walking astronauts use to enter and exit the orbiter without causing a catastrophic loss of cabin pressure.

To minimize the weight of the orbiter, the crew compartment is small. At 2,325 cubic feet, it's about the size of a small bedroom. Recalling one of his three shuttle flights, made between 1984 and 1990, astronaut Mike Mullane says:

> To better appreciate how tight the shuttle's quarters are, imagine being with five people (who haven't had a shower) for two weeks in a 100-square foot room (the approximate living area of our mid deck). If you want an even more vivid mental picture of the situation, imagine you are clamped to the toilet [astronauts have to fasten themselves to the commode in the weightlessness of space] in a call of nature while somebody is six feet away preparing supper.[1]

But, Mullane adds, cramped as the living and working area is, it's not as unbearable as a compartment of similar dimensions would be on Earth because the astronauts are not confined to the floor, but can make use of the entire volume. In weightlessness it's possible to sit on the ceiling, take a nap snuggled in an upper corner, or eat lunch floating in the middle of the capsule.

Thanks to the shuttle, astronauts can not only survive in the otherwise deadly environment of space; they can live and work there almost as easily and comfortably as they can on Earth. The shuttle has extended the frontiers of human exploration beyond the confines of the planet's atmosphere. It has also served as an important step in the creation of more long-term space habitats, like the International Space Station, that will one day culminate in permanent bases on the moon and Mars.

Training a Shuttle Crew

Each shuttle mission has a different crew. For them, life on board the spacecraft actually begins two years before they blast off. During that twenty-four-month period, the crew, comprising from three to seven astronauts (the average number is five), completes a rigorous three-stage training program: basic training on all aspects of shuttle operation, including emergency procedures; intermediate training to deepen their understanding of the shuttle and NASA's operating procedures; and mission-specific training to equip them to perform the jobs they'll have to do when they are in space. The training takes place in realistic mock-ups of the shuttle and utilizes sophisticated computer simulations. The stated goal of the training program is to confront the astronauts with every possible contingency they might encounter during the mission so they'll be able to function with machinelike efficiency in difficult circumstances. The implied goal is to forge them into a team whose survival depends on how well each of its members performs.

During training astronauts simulate the jobs they will perform in space.

How to Become a Shuttle Astronaut

Even before training begins, officials at NASA try to assure themselves that the corps of astronauts is composed of men and women who, in agency terminology, have the "right stuff" to be space travelers.

NASA does not recruit astronauts for shuttle missions. Those who wish to fly in space must take the initiative and submit an application, and any American citizen can apply. (Foreign astronauts have flown on the shuttle during multinational missions—like building the International Space Station, for example—but they were not considered NASA personnel.) Civilians can apply directly to NASA at any time; military personnel must submit their applications to review boards composed of officers from their particular branch of the armed services. All applications are scrutinized by a panel of veteran astronauts and senior NASA officials. This panel meets approximately every two years and chooses which applicants will be invited to the Johnson Space Center in Houston, Texas, for physical and psychological examinations and face-to-face interviews. The number of candidates chosen at this stage of the selection process depends on NASA's assessment of how many astronauts it will need in the near future. Usually, they will call five or six times as many candidates as they plan to accept into the training program. The exact number depends on the schedule of flights projected over the next two- or three-year period. It's not easy to become an astronaut. For example, in 1978—the year Sally Ride, who would go on to become the first American woman in space, applied to the program—there were a total of eight thousand applicants. Of these, thirty-five were accepted.

The basic physical requirements to be an astronaut are broad. While there is no age requirement, the academic qualifications needed mean that applicants will be at least in their early twenties. As of late 2001, the youngest, Tony England, was twenty-five when he became a member of the astronaut corps. The oldest, John Phillips, was forty-five. The average age is thirty-four. Candidates must be between four feet ten and a half inches and six feet four inches tall (pilots must be at least five feet four inches so they can reach all the shuttle's controls). There are no official weight restrictions. There have been female astronauts who weighed as little as a hundred pounds and men who have weighed as much as 220 pounds. It's permissible to wear glasses or contact lenses, but color-blind candidates are rejected because many of the switches and displays on the control panels are color-coded. Candidates must be in good health. Chronic medical conditions, such as heart disease or high blood pressure, are disqualifying conditions, as are ailments—asthma, for example—that require regular therapy or medication.

The physical examination is similar to that prescribed for private pilots by the Federal Aviation Administration. It includes a treadmill test and an EEG brain scan. About 85 percent of applicants pass the exam. Florida senator Bill Nelson, who flew on the shuttle in 1986, says: "Today's astronauts don't have to be super athletes. The shuttle offers a relatively benign environment that makes it possible to place everyday people into orbit. . . . But it does take stamina to perform several days of experiments in microgravity; naturally, being in top physical shape makes it easier."[2]

Educational criteria and technical skills are somewhat more specific. Candidates must have at least a bachelor's degree in science, mathematics, or engineering. Most chosen astronauts have advanced degrees in these fields. Only those who aspire to sit at the flight controls are required to have piloting skills. Although anyone with a thousand hours of jet pilot experience will be considered, most successful applicants have graduated from military test pilot academies. The rest of the crew are known as mission specialists, and they are required to have only the academic qualifications mentioned above.

Candidates are examined by two psychiatrists to determine their emotional fitness for spaceflight. The qualities considered important include the ability to react calmly in stressful situations, a willingness to follow orders, and the capacity to live and work harmoniously with members of the opposite sex and people of other races and cultural backgrounds. Some astronauts find the psychiatric exam humorous. Mike Mullane recalls:

> Some of the questions they asked are, "If you died, what epitaph would be etched on your tomb?" (If you said "Good Riddance" it would probably cast a shadow on your selection potential) and, "After death, if you could come back as an animal, what type of animal would you want to be?" (Almost everybody said an eagle or a falcon. A wish to be reincarnated as an aardvark probably wouldn't denote an astronaut disposition.)[3]

More important than the psychiatric evaluation in the selection process is the candidate interview, which is conducted by experienced astronauts who have firsthand knowledge of the personality traits necessary to be a productive shuttle crew member. The question-and-answer session takes an hour, and the examiners are primarily interested in whether or not the applicant has the characteristics exhibited by good team players. Candidates who exhibit traits like arrogance or an excessive need to

control others are weeded out. Shuttle missions require good communication and the ability to work well with other people. Since each launch involves risk to human life and hundreds of millions of dollars worth of equipment, NASA is rigorous in attempting to eliminate personality conflict as a potential source of error.

Astronaut Scott J. Horowitz practices a parachute drop into water, an important safety technique.

Basic Training

Those candidates who survive the application and selection process begin a year of basic training at the Johnson Space Center. The instructional facilities are set up like a university campus. The faculty is comprised of approximately 160 training personnel, and they are stern taskmasters. Shuttle systems are far more complex than those of earlier spacecraft, and astronaut candidates have to be thoroughly trained in their operation. Thus, the training program has to be both thorough and rigorous, and the training staff is under-

standably intolerant of student error. Every procedure is practiced repetitively until it becomes second nature—no laziness or inattention is permitted under any circumstances.

Astronaut candidates (or ASCANs, as they are called) attend a full range of formal academic courses in mathematics, meteorology, navigation, astronomy, physics, space medicine, and computer science. They also practice aircraft safety, including ejection, parachuting, survival in hostile environments, and other emergency procedures. Through lectures, textbooks, flight operations manuals, and training in realistic mock-ups of the orbiter, they become familiar with the shuttle and how its many complicated systems work. They also train in T-38 aircraft, the planes in which military jet fighter pilots hone their skills: those who intend to become shuttle pilots learn to fly these high-performance jets; mission specialists are acclimatized to supersonic (faster than the speed of sound) flight by riding as passengers. Since the shuttle lands on a runway, much as an airplane does, pilot astronauts practice landing procedures in a modified Grumman Gulfstream II jet that has been adapted to simulate the touchdown characteristics of the orbiter.

The ASCANs also accustom themselves to weightlessness and prepare for space walks in the world's largest indoor swimming pool. Space journalist G. Harry Stine describes this facility:

It holds 1,300,000 gallons of water, is 75 feet in diameter, and has a depth of 40 feet. Full-scale mock-ups of spacecraft and space modules can be placed in it. Space-suited astronauts using special life-support backpacks and weighted to achieve neutral buoyancy can work in the tank and feel as if they were in weightlessness. They're monitored by scuba divers. This is the closest simulation to weightlessness that can be achieved in the persistent gravity of Earth.[4]

In the pool the astronauts painstakingly practice all the ordinary tasks they may be called upon to do in space. They also drill on emergency procedures. Working in the tank can itself be dangerous. In *Before Lift-Off: The Making of a Space Shuttle Crew*, space historian Henry Cooper explains: "There is

The Johnson Space Center houses the largest indoor swimming pool in the world. The pool simulates the weightlessness of space.

always [an ambulance] parked by the pool when astronauts are in it. Though there has never been a serious accident, there have been some close calls. . . . The astronauts in their suits cannot swim; the divers have to move them, fetch for them, and be on the lookout for trouble."[5] While training for an early shuttle mission, astronaut James van Hoften came close to death when an oxygen hose pulled out of his suit. The divers sprang into action and had him up a ladder, out of the water, and his helmet off in thirty seconds.

Divers are on hand to rescue astronauts during underwater training.

A KC-135 airplane creates conditions designed to give trainees the feeling of weightlessness.

The Vomit Comet

As a further introduction to weightlessness, the ASCANs are flown aboard a KC-135 airplane (similar to a Boeing 707 jetliner with all the seats removed). To create the right conditions for weightlessness to occur, the plane dives steeply to pick up speed, pulls up abruptly, climbs rapidly, and then plunges downward for about twenty to twenty-five seconds until its velocity exceeds the acceleration produced by Earth's gravitational force (thirty-two feet per second squared). "Things just start to float off

the floor," says veteran astronaut William Pogue, who has flown many times on the KC-135. "The cabin, the people, and all the equipment behave as if in space weightlessness. . . . During a single training session the KC-135, also referred to as the K-Bird, may execute over fifty of these pull-up and push-over maneuvers. After several of these maneuvers some people develop nausea."[6]

In fact, upset stomachs are so common during the breathtaking climbs and dives, the astronauts have nicknamed the KC-135 the "Vomit Comet." Although each episode of weightlessness lasts less than half a minute, it provides the astronauts with enough time to practice simple tasks. Senator Bill Nelson says his first experience in zero gravity made him feel like a Ping-Pong ball. "When I felt the plane dip and my body lighten, I unstrapped and pushed off—too hard," he says. "I sailed upward, crashing into the ceiling. But before long, and with some practice, I was effortlessly turning flips. It took very controlled movements and a soft touch to keep from ping-ponging off the walls of the plane."[7]

Diet and Exercise

NASA does not prescribe a physical training program for the ASCANs. They are expected to stay in good condition, but how they do so is left to personal choice. "NASA's only health requirement is that astronauts be able to pass their physical exams," says Mike Mullane. "How an astronaut stays in shape to pass this checkup is entirely up to the individual. Most astronauts exercise regularly by jogging and playing racquet sports, but the only exercise some engage in is walking to the door to pay the pizza delivery person." Nor is there a special diet. "I have seen astronauts eat a vending machine lunch of a Diet Coke and a Twinkie," Mullane says, "while others have had beer and peanut suppers."[8]

Nevertheless, most of the ASCANs opt to eat healthy meals and work out regularly. They quickly learn that their long and demanding training sessions require them to be in peak physical and mental condition. Bill Nelson describes how he started every day during his training program: "During the first week I found myself falling into a regular routine. . . . Before I went to the Space Center at 7:30 A.M., I would run, do some calisthenics, and eat a breakfast of grapefruit, rolled oats,

and apple juice."[9] Almost all other ASCANs adopt a similar regimen, and most of them maintain it for as long as they remain members of the astronaut corps.

Apart from running and racquet sports, some astronauts choose to stay fit by cycling, weight training, mountain climbing, and practicing martial arts. To build team spirit, they are encouraged to exercise together as often as they can. They also socialize with one another to cement the bonds that will enable them to live and work together in close quarters when they are chosen for shuttle missions.

During basic training, ASCANs are given the opportunity to learn a second language to facilitate good communication with astronauts from other countries. Most study Russian, since Russia is America's principal partner in building the International Space

Station. Many astronauts feel that knowing Russian improves their chances of being selected for missions. Others choose to learn Japanese, French, or German—astronauts from all these countries are expected to play significant roles in the space station's future.

Intermediate Training

After the ASCANs complete their basic training, they are assigned to ground duties, called job assignments, while waiting to be picked for a specific shuttle mission. During this period, which normally lasts several months, they evaluate equipment that NASA plans to use on future flights and help the design engineers make it more user-friendly.

The ASCANs also take sixteen different courses covering all aspects of shuttle operation, including navigation, control systems, and payload deployment and retrieval. Most of this training takes place in what NASA refers to as low- and medium-fidelity training equipment—specialized flight simulators that permit the astronauts to learn at their own pace by interacting with computer programs. The goal of this part of the training program, the space agency says, is to "provide instruction in orbiter systems. It is not related to a specific mission or its cargo. It is designed to familiarize the trainee with a feel for what it's like to work and live in space."[10]

In all, the ASCANs spend about a thousand to fifteen hundred hours in these simulators. Individual sessions can last as long as eight hours, and instructors keep them on their toes by manipulating the software to stage malfunctions—some of them minor, some of them major—to perfect their ability to respond quickly and calmly to unexpected situations that could put their lives and the lives of their fellow crew members in jeopardy.

It is at this stage that the ASCANs become fully acquainted with the vast team of people required to make each shuttle mission

Astronaut Edward T. Lu tries on a training version of a shuttle launch-and-entry garment.

a success. "Career astronauts cannot afford the luxury of specializing in one particular field of knowledge," explains astronaut David Leestma.

Instead, the crew members become highly trained generalists. In preparing to be such generalists, they depend heavily upon numerous other people who will take part in this mission—people like the training personnel, the flight controllers, the contractors [the aerospace corporations who built the shuttle and maintain the shuttle], the design engineers, and the mission managers.[11]

Mission-Specific Training

When an astronaut is chosen for a mission, his or her training shifts to the Shuttle Mission Simulator (SMS), a $100 million, high-fidelity replica of the orbiter designed to mimic all phases of a shuttle flight, from liftoff to touchdown. "All the controls, and all the instrumentation, are hooked up to big Univac and IBM computers that can be programmed to duplicate entire missions or any parts of them," says space journalist Henry Cooper, who followed the crew of the forty-first shuttle mission through their training program.

Even the views out the windows—computer-generated graphics that appear on screens—are realistic: astronauts see the earth below or fields of stars; out the rear windows, they see the payload bay and its contents. In addition to the sights, they experience the sounds of space flight: the thump of attitude-control jets firing, the hum of a caution-and-warning alarm, the buzz of a master alarm.[12]

The Shuttle Mission Simulator is designed to mimic all phases of a shuttle flight.

The SMS is really two simulators, one motion-based and the other fixed. The motion-based simulator, says Cooper, "is used mainly for practicing ascents and descents, and it swivels in all directions—it can tip upright and vibrate, to give the feelings of launch, and it can twist this way and that, to give the feeling of an aircraft banking in the atmosphere on its way home."[13] The fixed simulator is configured with functional versions of all the systems and workstations the astronauts will use to carry out their mission in space.

During the hundreds of hours they spend together in the SMS, the shuttle crew becomes a fully integrated team. As they practice their tasks over and over again, they learn each other's work and speech habits, quirks and foibles, strengths and weaknesses. They also learn each other's jobs so they can fill in should an emergency require it.

"A team works well when they all know how each will react in different sets of circumstances," say veteran shuttle commander Robert Crippen. "We have to develop mutual trust. And we do this in the simulators. A crew matures a bit when it's been in the simulators. Simulators are a closed environment where we're stressed. You cannot handle malfunctions without working together as a crew, and the simulators allow us to do that."[14]

Emergency Training

As the launch date approaches, the mission control personnel who will be on duty on the ground during the flight are integrated into the simulations so that they will be able to work seamlessly with the astronauts in space. Together, they learn how to deal with both routine and unexpected events. During these sessions, instructors sitting at consoles in another room cause various pieces of equipment to fail to judge how the crew and mission controllers react.

"The training is brutal—particularly launch training," says Mike Mullane.

It's during ascent that things happen so fast any mistake could be disastrous, so astronauts and mission controllers are really stressed with failures during simulated launches. The instructors might simulate an engine failure at 1 minute into flight, a hydraulic failure at 1 minute 30 seconds, an electrical failure at 2 minutes, a navigation failure at 2 minutes 30 seconds, a computer failure at 3 minutes, a fuel leak at 3 minutes 30 seconds, and so on. The individuals who prepare these training scenarios are called sim sups, for simulation supervisors. Astronauts joke the sim sups wear starched underwear and shoes that are two sizes too small so they can make themselves mean as snakes and dream up all manner of diabolical failures.[15]

The astronauts spend eight to twelve hours a week in the SMS for the entire year they are preparing for their mission, more time than they spend on any other aspect of their training. They are so painstakingly and repetitively drilled that many of them say actual spaceflight is a snap by comparison. "In the simulators, they gave us malf [malfunction] after malf in a way that is completely unrealistic," says David Leestma. "Coming out of those sessions, you felt completely beat down."[16]

But Mullane defends the grueling training by citing an incident that occurred shortly after he blasted off on his first space mission. President Ronald Reagan placed a phone call through a satellite linkup to congratulate the astronauts. During the conversation, an emergency alarm sounded. Rather than cut

Mission Control

Every shuttle flight has an unseen crew, hundreds of men and women on the mission control team who support the astronauts from computer terminals in the Flight Control Room at the Johnson Space Center in Houston, Texas. Working around the clock in shifts, they monitor all of the astronauts' activities and every one of the shuttle's many complex systems to ensure that the mission they are responsible for is both safe and successful.

The flight director heads up the flight control team and is responsible for overall shuttle and payload operations. He or she has ultimate authority, even over that of the commander of the mission, for the safety and conduct of the vessel from the moment it clears the launch tower at the Kennedy Space Center in Florida until it lands.

The spacecraft communicator, usually a member of the astronaut corps, is the principal link between the shuttle crew and mission control. Other officers are responsible for specific aspects of the mission, for example, the robotic arm, space walks, cargo, and so on. In addition, the mission control team is supported by a group of engineers, computer programmers, and other technical experts.

The mission control team monitors the activities of a space mission from the Flight Control Room at the Johnson Space Center.

the call short, some of the astronauts continued to chat with the president while others calmly carried out well-practiced troubleshooting procedures. One of the crew members identified the problem by running a computerized diagnostic program. Then several others floated over to the control panel that governed the failing system and carried out the required repairs. The event was handled so routinely that even the astronauts struggling with the problem were able to say a few words to Reagan while they were busy working. The president didn't realize a crisis had occurred—and been resolved—until after the telephone conversation was over.

The purpose of the grueling training program is to guarantee that shuttle astronauts will be able to deal with any emergency that could possibly arise. The diligence has paid off. During the spacecraft's first one hundred flights, crew members were able to overcome numerous problems while in orbit. Only one malfunction, the one that destroyed the *Challenger* in 1986, ever resulted in loss of life or even forced a mission to terminate before its principal objectives were accomplished.

CHAPTER 2

Blastoff

Shuttle astronauts are unanimous on one point: blastoff is the greatest adrenaline rush they've ever experienced. Lying on their backs, strapped into their seats on the uptilted orbiter, they patiently wait as the seconds tick by. Then, less than two hundred feet beneath them, 3.8 million pounds of rocket fuel explodes with a deafening roar. The shuttle trembles as 6 million pounds of thrust slowly lift it off the launchpad. Ten and a half breathtaking minutes later, the astronauts are traveling at almost eighteen thousand miles an hour, floating weightlessly in space.

Launch Day

Several days before liftoff, the astronauts fly from the training facility in Houston to the Kennedy Space Center at Cape Canaveral on Florida's east coast. They are put in quarantine to prevent them from coming in contact with anyone suffering from an infectious condition; a severe case of the flu might be enough to delay a $400 million mission. Their quarters are spartan. Each gets a ten-by-twelve-foot room sparsely furnished with a dark blue carpet, a double bed, a lamp, a telephone, two small dressers, a bookcase, and a mirror. Astronauts admit that the room is far from luxurious, but most of them find it adequate for their needs. They agree with NASA's policy of spending its limited resources on making the shuttle safe and efficient, rather than on making them comfortable while they are on the ground. Besides, they all concur, in the days before a launch, they are usually too excited to pay much attention to their surroundings.

While the astronauts were training at the Johnson Space Center, an army of technicians was putting in forty thousand man-hours of work doing more than ten thousand separate tasks during a sixty-five-day period to get the shuttle ready to fly. Now the moment has arrived. On launch day the astronauts are awakened five hours before liftoff. They shower and eat a light breakfast. In the 1960s, when the space program was in its infancy, NASA distributed publicity photos showing the astronauts eating hearty steak-and-eggs breakfasts to convey a macho image. Today the shuttle crew goes into space with as little in their stomachs as possible to avoid—not always successfully—having to evacuate their bladders and bowels when the gravitational forces of liftoff press on their abdomens.

After breakfast the astronauts suit up. The first thing they put on is a urine collection device, essentially an adult diaper for women and a condomlike attachment for men. Next they don long underwear and high socks. Technicians help them into orange pressure suits and boots. The inflatable suit has two functions: it maintains normal atmospheric pressure on the body during the shuttle's ascent into orbit; and it can also function as a flotation device should the astronauts have to bail out into the ocean.

Then the crew is driven nine miles to the launchpad. Sally Ride, who flew on the shuttle in 1983 and 1984, describes the experience:

An astronaut dons his launch-and-entry suit with help from an assistant.

The space shuttle stands with its nose pointed toward the sky, attached to the big orange fuel tank and two white rockets that will lift it—and us—into space. The spotlights shining on the space shuttle light the last part of our route. . . . When we step out onto the pad, we're dwarfed by the 30-story-high space shuttle. Our space plane looked peaceful from the road, but now we can hear it hissing and gurgling as though it's alive.[17]

The Long Wait

The astronauts ride an elevator to the White Room, a retractable chamber that joins the shuttle to the launch tower, 195 feet above the ground, where six technicians are waiting to help them into their escape harnesses, parachutes, and launch helmets, and assist them as they clamber through the orbiter's small circular hatch and into their seats. Because the shuttle stands tail downward, they lie on their backs with their faces pointing up toward the vessel's nose. Getting seated is awkward because the gear they're wearing weighs a total of eighty-three pounds. Then begins a seemingly endless one-and-a-half-hour wait until the engines ignite.

The commander and pilot are busy doing preflight checks, but the mission specialists have nothing to occupy them except listening to the eerie sounds emanating from the spacecraft. "I was conscious of how 'alive' the space ship seemed to be," says Bill Nelson.

Now, strapped into the bowels of the great animal, I could hear its body sounds—the circulation of its fluids, the groaning and creaking of the skeleton, the slurping sounds of liquids and gasses moving through the miles of pipes and tubes. The ship seemed to be breathing deeply, as a runner at the blocks inhales and exhales to prepare his lungs for the race.[18]

The astronauts admit that the thousands of hours they spend in the simulators during

Because space shuttles stand with their tails to the ground, astronauts must lie on their backs during blastoff.

training are not enough to prepare them for the emotions they feel at this moment. "The adrenaline was pumping," says Jim McBride. "In sims, if things go wrong, we turn off the simulator and freeze the data. We can't do that here."[19] The specter of the *Challenger* explosion that claimed the lives of seven astronauts in 1986 looms large. Even before that tragedy occurred, the astronauts harbored no illusions that they were not involved in an extremely high-risk adventure. Nelson, who flew several months before the *Challenger* disaster, found himself silently repeating the Twenty-third Psalm. "The night before, most of our crew had ended up in the sauna to try to relax before we went to bed," he says.

We started talking about all the things that could go wrong—and, of course, there were many. . . . If we lost two of our three engines during the first seven and a half minutes of the ascent, we would not be able to make an emergency landing and would have to try ditching in the ocean. It was clearly understood by all of us that we probably would not survive the impact of the water. In fact, the more I thought about it, the more I became aware of the mission as an enormous interlocking web of calculated risks, any one of which could prove fatal. . . . Were we operating on borrowed time, as many of the astronauts suspected? Or, had the

The Challenger *lifts off (left) and explodes (right). The explosion that killed seven astronauts became a reminder of the potential dangers of space travel.*

Twenty minutes before liftoff, control of the shuttle shifts from ground computers to those on board.

technical ability of NASA become so practiced that a mission like ours was now simply a matter of routine? Lying on my back in the shuttle, I wondered.[20]

All Systems Go

Thirty minutes before liftoff, the ground crew withdraws to the White Room. Ten minutes later an alarm sounds, indicating that control of the shuttle has been shifted from ground computers to those on board. (NASA counts down to the launch in minus numbers. After liftoff, which occurs at T minus zero, time is measured in positive numbers.) At T minus ten minutes, there is an automatic hold for a final check of all the systems. But this is rarely the

only hold; other delays—due to weather or to fix minor technical problems—frequently add to the astronauts' anxiety and discomfort.

"I was strapped into the cockpit of the space shuttle *Atlantis* waiting my third and final mission into space," says Mike Mullane.

My body was in agony. We were at T minus nine minutes and holding. Bad weather had already postponed the launch for an hour beyond the intended lift-off time, and we had been in the cockpit for almost three hours. The steel chair, the lumpy parachute, and stiff pressure suit were all conspiring to torture my back. I arched my back to relieve some of the worst pressure points. The 83 pounds of equipment that enveloped me made the

The *Challenger* Disaster

The most dangerous part of a shuttle mission is the liftoff. This fact was burned into the national consciousness on January 28, 1986, when millions of television spectators watched in stunned horror as the *Challenger*, one of four orbiters in the shuttle fleet, exploded into an orange-and-red fireball, claiming the lives of seven astronauts.

At fifty-two seconds into the flight, the spacecraft had reached an altitude of 4.9 miles above the Kennedy Space Center in Florida and was traveling at nineteen hundred miles per hour. Mission control told commander Dick Scobee that the onboard computers were about to throttle the main engines up to full power. He radioed back: "Roger, go at throttle up." Those were the last words transmitted from the *Challenger*.

Twenty-three seconds later, a seal, called an O-ring, on the right solid rocket booster failed, allowing flaming gases to escape. The intensely hot gases burned through the liquid fuel tank, to which the solid rocket booster was bolted, causing the hydrogen and oxygen it contained to erupt in a cataclysmic explosion.

On the ground and on television sets around the world, spectators saw the *Challenger* engulfed in a massive ball of fire. Then they witnessed smoke trails as fragments of the shattered spacecraft plunged toward the Atlantic Ocean.

With eerie calm, the NASA announcer, Steven Nesbitt, said over the public address system that there appeared to have been "a major malfunction." After several seconds of silence, he added: "We have a report from the flight dynamics officer that the vehicle has exploded. The flight director confirms that. We are looking at checking with recovery forces to see what can be done at this point."

Nothing could be done. The seven astronauts, including teacher Christa McAuliffe, died on impact when the crew compartment hit the water. It is believed they were conscious up to that point.

The disaster prompted President Ronald Reagan to cancel all shuttle flights and appoint a commission to inquire into the causes of the explosion. The commission, which included astronaut Sally Ride among its members, concluded that the O-ring failed because the temperature at launch time was too cold (it was twenty-eight degrees). They also faulted NASA executives for ignoring warnings that the low temperature would impair the proper functioning of the ring.

Shuttle flights resumed two years later, after design and procedural modifications recommended by the commission were implemented.

---

movement a struggle, but the momentary restoration of circulation was heaven-sent. But the relief was brief. As my muscles fatigued and my body sagged back into the seat, I could feel a puddle of cold urine rising around my crotch. It was being squeezed from my urine collection device. "Now I know why babies cry when their diapers are wet," I thought. The feeling was disgusting.[21]

At T minus two minutes, the astronauts shut the visors of their helmets and activate their emergency oxygen supplies. "I could now hear my fear in the hissing sound of my accelerated breathing," Mullane says. "The last call from the Launch Director: 'Good luck and godspeed, *Atlantis*.' T minus 30 seconds. Except for the soft whooshing background noise of the cabin fans, the cockpit was deathly quiet. T minus 10 seconds. My heart choked me. I tried to swallow, but I had no saliva."[22]

Liftoff

As the countdown continues, the crew feels the shuttle shudder slightly as the computers swivel the main engines into launch position. At T minus six seconds, the engines ignite. The shuttle, still bolted to the launchpad, sways forty inches from vertical and then suddenly snaps back to an upright position, a maneuver called "twanging." It's a crucial moment: while the main engines roar, the ship's computers do a final scan of the solid rocket boosters. Once these powerful rockets ignite, there is no turning back. The shuttle begins to vibrate violently as it strains at the bolts holding it to the launchpad. The fate of the vessel and its crew

Aborts

The two-minute-twenty-second period between the moment when the solid rocket boosters ignite and when they burn out and detach from the shuttle is the most perilous time in any shuttle mission. If a catastrophic malfunction occurs during this time—as happened when the *Challenger* blew up in 1986—the astronauts accept that there is almost no chance they will survive.

Following the separation of the solid rocket boosters, the shuttle is powered by its three main engines, which run on liquid fuel contained in the big orange tank. Should difficulty arise at this stage of the ascent, there are a number of options available to abort the flight and return the astronauts safely. Only the fourth of these procedures has ever been implemented, and NASA admits the others have—at best—only a small chance of succeeding.

Return to Launch Site (RTLS): If the engines malfunction very soon after the solid rocket boosters have separated, the shuttle continues along its flight path until it has just enough fuel left for the commander to turn it around. He then jettisons the big orange liquid fuel tank, glides back to the launch site at the Kennedy Space Center, and attempts to land the shuttle as he would do at the end of a successful mission.

Trans-Atlantic Abort (TAL): After liftoff the shuttle flies in an easterly direction across the Atlantic Ocean. If it has gone far enough before the problem occurs, the commander attempts to land it at one of several emergency sites, located in Germany, Spain, Morocco, and Senegal.

Abort Once Around (AOA): This option is available if the malfunction strikes when the shuttle has attained enough velocity to make it to an emergency landing site in White Sands, New Mexico. The main fuel tank is jettisoned, and the commander uses the orbiter's onboard maneuvering engines to maintain enough altitude so that the craft can fly once around Earth before he attempts a landing.

Abort to Orbit (ATO): If the main engines fail very late in the shuttle's ascent, the craft can attain a low orbit around Earth. The commander then uses the onboard engines to gradually increase the altitude, and if everything goes right, the mission can sometimes be completed as planned. If not, the shuttle orbits once or twice and then lands as it would at the end of a successful mission.

shifts from human hands at the launch control center to the onboard computers, which scan the engines for malfunctions. The seconds tick down—three, two, one—the solid rockets fire, explosives shatter the restraining bolts, and the shuttle begins its ascent.

The shock wave from the combustion of the solid rocket fuel can be felt three miles away. Explosive charges shatter the bolts holding the shuttle to the launchpad, and the spaceship lifts off the ground in a cloud of flame. "Inside, the ride is rough and loud," Sally Ride says. "Our heads are rattling around inside our helmets. We can barely hear the voices from mission control in our headsets above the thunder of the rockets and engines. For an instant I wonder if everything is working right. But there's no more time to wonder, and no time to be scared."[23]

The shuttle starts its journey into space with majestic slowness, but in seconds it begins to accelerate rapidly. "There was a jolt and a huge roar," says Bill Nelson.

I pulled my hands back up against my chest and turned my head to the left so I could see out of the window. Everything was gray. It was the gray steel of the [launch] tower, and I could see it sliding by the window as we began our ascent. I was astounded at how quickly we were moving, slow at first then faster with each second. It took only four seconds to clear the tower, the engines burning furiously. As we cleared the tower, I could see the ground illuminated by the fire of the motors. The next view from the window was darkness, then the lights of Cape Canaveral. . . . Sud-

Flames and exhaust scatter as a shuttle begins its ascent.

denly, I felt a tremendous kick, a surge of energy as I was pinned on my back.[24]

At T plus five seconds, oversight of the shuttle is transferred from launch control in Florida to mission control at the Johnson Space Center in Houston. Two seconds later the craft begins a rollover maneuver to set it on the right flight path. At this point it is flying upside down, with the fuel tank on top and the orbiter beneath. Its speed is a hundred miles per hour, and the g forces on the astronauts' bodies are building.

Higher and Faster

Thirty seconds after liftoff, the g forces reach their maximum. The shuttle begins to shake violently, and the astronauts are forced back into their seats as three times the normal weight of the atmosphere bears down on their chests. Although the pressure is so strong the crew members have difficulty breathing and can barely turn their heads, they have experienced greater g forces during training. But these lasted for only a few seconds. During an actual launch, minute after minute passes by with no relief from the distressing feeling that many crew members describe as having an elephant sitting on your chest. Even veteran astronauts admit that they find themselves longing for weightlessness during this part of the launch.

At T plus two minutes and eight seconds, the astronauts hear a thud and feel the shuttle lurch as explosive charges blow the bolts that hold the solid rocket boosters to the external fuel tank. "I was startled by the huge jolt as they broke loose," Nelson says.

Suddenly, it was quiet as the SRBs [solid rocket boosters], still burning fiercely from their tails, slipped away. . . . For a moment I was puzzled at the lack of noise; then I remembered we were flying faster than the speed of sound and the exhaust of our main engines was behind us. Our speed was increasing toward our maximum of 17,795 miles per hour.[25]

As the velocity of the shuttle continues to rise, the main engines are throttled down to 65 percent of their maximum power to maintain the pressure on the astronauts' bodies at three g's. "Although I had experienced g forces in the supersonic jets, these were stronger than I expected," Nelson says. "I strained against them by tightening my stomach. . . . I realized it was because I was on my back, and the force was sustained for almost two minutes."[26]

At T plus eight minutes and thirty-eight seconds, the shuttle achieves orbital velocity. In that brief time, it has consumed almost 4 million pounds of solid and liquid rocket fuel—an average of more than seven thousand pounds per second—and accelerated from zero miles per hour to six times the speed of a high-powered rifle bullet. A few seconds later, the large orange liquid fuel tank separates from the vessel and tumbles down into the atmosphere, where the forces of friction cause it to break up and burn. Disencumbered from the tank and the solid rocket boosters, the shuttle is now a free-flying space plane.

Weightless!

As soon as the main fuel tank separates, the shuttle ceases to vibrate and becomes completely quiet. It is now being powered by the silent forces of Earth's gravity and its own velocity. It has become an Earth satellite, governed by the same physical laws that keep the moon in its orbit. It is at this point that the astronauts get their first taste of weightlessness.

"Instantly, the g forces disappeared, replaced just as suddenly by weightlessness," Nelson says.

Now in zero gravity, still strapped to my seat, I stared in wonderment as my arms started floating at chest level right in front of my eyes. I glanced over at Franklin [mission specialist Franklin Diaz, one of Nelson's crewmates]. His arms were floating, too. Debris on the cabin floor, which had shaken loose during the vibrations of the ascent, was starting to float up. . . . I felt a mixture of gratitude and disbelief.[27]

Sally Ride adds: "The launch engines cut off. Suddenly, the force is gone, and we lurch forward in our seats. During the next few minutes, the empty fuel tank drops away and falls to Earth, and we are busy getting the shuttle ready . . . but we're not too busy to notice that our books and pencils are floating in midair. We are in space!"[28]

Although the shuttle is in orbit, the commander and pilot have to execute one more maneuver. The orbit at this point is an ellipse (an elongated oval) with a high point, or apogee, of about 185 miles above Earth's surface and a low point, or perigee, of about forty miles. The perigee is too low for the shuttle to maintain its orbit—atmospheric density at that altitude is still great enough to slow the vessel down. The two orbital maneuvering system engines burn for a few minutes, in-

The payload bay doors of the Atlantis *open after the shuttle is in orbit. By this time, astronauts feel the weightlessness of space.*

The Shuttle Fleet

There are four orbiters in the shuttle fleet: *Columbia, Discovery, Atlantis,* and *Endeavor.* Each cost approximately $1.1 billion to build.

Columbia was completed in 1979 and on April 12, 1982, became the first shuttle to fly into orbit. It is named after a small sailing vessel that operated out of Boston in 1792 and explored the mouth of the Columbia River.

Discovery was pronounced flight-ready in 1983 and undertook its first mission on August 30, 1984. It is named after two famous sailing ships: the one captained by Henry Hudson while the explorer was searching for the Northwest Passage in 1610 and 1611; and the vessel commanded by James Cook when he discovered the Hawaiian Islands in 1778.

Atlantis took its maiden flight in April 1985. It takes its name from a ship that undertook scientific investigations for the Woods Hole Oceanographic Institution between the years 1930 and 1966.

Endeavor, named after another of explorer James Cook's vessels, was commissioned in 1987 to replace *Challenger,* which was destroyed a year earlier. It was launched for the first time in 1992.

In addition to these four fully operational orbiters (and the ill-fated *Challenger*), NASA also had an additional vehicle, identical to the others except that it was not equipped with engines and electronics, that was used in aerodynamic tests in the late 1970s. This ship was named by the American people in a poll conducted by the space agency. They chose to call it *Enterprise,* after the vessel in the *Star Trek* TV series and movies, and it now resides at the Smithsonian Institution in Washington, D.C.

Discovery is one of four orbiters in the shuttle fleet.

creasing the speed of the shuttle slightly and raising it into a near-circular orbit about two hundred miles (the exact altitude varies from mission to mission) above Earth.

At that point the astronauts experience a profound sense of relief. They know, from their training and the experience of the *Challenger* explosion, that liftoff is the most perilous part of any shuttle mission. Also, even though astronauts often fly on more than one mission during their careers at NASA, there are usually at least one or two rookies on every flight, and this is the first moment when they have the opportunity to savor the sensation of extended weightlessness. To break the tension, mission control transmits a lighthearted message welcoming the newcomers to space. The respite is brief, however. Soon the astronauts will be hard at work.

Adapting to Microgravity

As soon as the shuttle reaches the orbit it will follow for the rest of the mission, the astronauts swing into action. Since only the seats occupied by the commander and the pilot are permanently bolted to the floor of the cockpit, the mission specialists have to stow theirs away to make room for working and living during the flight. They also have to gather up books, clipboards, pens, and other paraphernalia, which are now floating freely about the cabin. Most importantly, they have to open the cargo bay doors so the heat radiators they contain can start to function. If they don't do this right away, the temperature inside the crew compartment will rise to dangerous levels. This flurry of activity, of course, occurs in a weightless environment, and the space travelers admit all the training they did in the pool and the Vomit Comet hasn't quite equipped them for the real experience.

First Impressions

As the astronauts are going about their work, they quickly become aware how different life without gravity is. Their first impression is the sudden absence of pressure on their bodies. After the g forces they experienced on liftoff, this is a welcome relief. But almost as quickly, they begin to feel light-headed and disoriented. Their faces feel hot and flushed, and the blood vessels in their necks pulsate noticeably. When they try to move, they tumble out of control. Many feel nauseated.

Microgravity

Even the astronauts themselves talk about life outside the influence of gravity. But technically the shuttle is never beyond the influence of Earth's gravitational field; in fact, it is Earth's gravity that keeps the shuttle circling around the planet in its orbit rather than flying off into space in a straight line.

The weightlessness astronauts experience stems from the fact that any orbiting object is in a state of free fall around Earth. Weight occurs when the force that gravity exerts on an object is countered by an opposing force. For example, when a person stands on a scale, gravity pulls his or her body downward, while the surface of the scale pushes upward with an equal force. In free fall there is no force to oppose that of gravity and, hence, objects are weightless.

Their sinus passages fill with fluid and their heads feel stuffy, as though they had colds. Most of them get a severe headache that often lasts for several hours, contributing to the feeling of nausea. Most of these symptoms begin to ease within a few hours, although some astronauts are bothered by them periodically during their entire time in space. This is particularly true of the sinus congestion, and many of the space travelers report a strong sensation of tumbling or spinning if they move their heads too quickly.

After adjusting to these early sensations, the astronauts remove their pressure suits and helmets. When they get their bearings and gaze around, they are struck by the fact that they not only feel very different in space, but they also look different. "Facial appearance changes quite a lot," says William Pogue, whose long career at NASA spanned both the era of Skylab, the first U.S. space station, and that of the shuttle.

I was really surprised—if not shocked—the first time I looked in the mirror. I didn't look like me anymore. Loose flesh on the face rises, or floats, on the bone structure, giving a high-cheekboned or Asian appearance. The face also looks a bit puffy, with bags under the eyes, especially during the first few days, and the veins in your forehead and neck appear swollen. After about three or four days, some of the facial puffiness and vein enlargement goes away, but your face still looks quite a bit different.[29]

The astronauts' eyes tend to bug out slightly, and their hair, if it is long enough, floats like a halo around their heads. Long hair is a potential safety hazard because it can get caught in air-intake vents or become entwined around switches and other pieces of equipment. Most women astronauts tie their hair into buns or pony-tails to minimize the risk.

Bill Nelson, who was not a career astronaut and hence somewhat less prepared for life in space than his fellow crew members, was startled by the profound effects of weightlessness. "Life at zero gravity has its own peculiar laws, and I at once began to notice changes," he says.

Most immediately my body fluids had started to shift out of my legs and into my upper torso. I looked around. Both Bob's and Franklin's [crewmates Bob Crippen and Franklin Diaz] faces had become red and puffy. I could feel the pressure in my own cheeks and realized I was puffing up like a chipmunk with a mouthful of acorns.

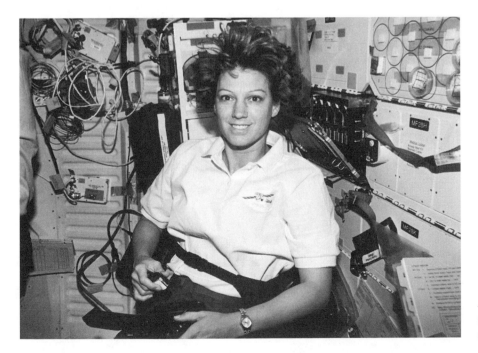

An astronaut's hair rises when the force of gravity is negated.

The sensation was like hanging upside down when all the blood rushes to your head—which is precisely what had happened. Well, actually, it hadn't all rushed to my head. It was simply being distributed evenly throughout my body, rather than heading for my feet, as it does on earth.[30]

Which Way Is Up?

Moving around the crew compartment, the astronauts become aware that the rules of Earth-bound motion no longer apply. By merely touching a wall, they could send their bodies catapulting across the cabin. Heavy objects, like the shuttle's ninety-seven-pound removable seats, became light as feathers. A lifting job that took two strong men on Earth could be accomplished effortlessly with one hand in space. The extreme ease of motion

had hidden dangers, and the astronauts were aware that they could easily break bones by crashing into a wall if they propelled themselves too quickly from place to place.

In designing the shuttle, NASA's engineers were careful to protect all important switches in the crew area with hoops or wickets so that a free-floating astronaut wouldn't inadvertently strike one with a wayward hand or foot. The orbiter is also equipped with many handholds and grips so that the astronauts can push and pull themselves safely from one position to another—and have something to grab onto in order to stop themselves before they crash into equipment or one another.

Simply distinguishing between up and down is a challenge in the absence of gravity. "It does take a little time to get used to weightlessness," Mullane explains. "For the first hour or so of my rookie mission, I found myself constantly fighting my body orienta-

Crew members float inside the shuttle. Distinguishing between up and down is difficult in space.

Pilot Charles O. Hobaugh prepares to do some work on the Atlantis *flight deck. He may be upside down for part of his work day.*

tion. I wanted my head toward the cockpit ceiling and my feet on the floor. After a while, the brain finally begins to accept the fact there is no up or down in orbit and you get used to being in all attitudes."[31]

Even sneezing can be a problem, as Pogue explains:

> The air rushes out your nose at about 100 miles per hour during a sneeze so it would act like a small jet or rocket and would propel you upward and rotate you backward. I performed a simple calculation based on my body size and the result was that a sneeze would cause me to do a complete backward somersault and move me about five feet upward.[32]

Orbital space flight is almost silent, and most of the astronauts relish the serene and peaceful atmosphere. When the main engines shut down, the only sound they hear is the gentle hum of the air conditioner's fans. They are struck by the fact that they are traveling at al-most eighteen thousand miles an hour, fast enough to circle Earth every ninety minutes, and yet have no sensation that the vessel they're in is moving at all—unless they look out one of the windows and see the planet's oceans and continents drifting across their field of vision.

Nothing's Easy

The astronauts discover that sitting down and bending over are very strenuous without the help of gravity. Their bodies naturally assume what is called "space neutral posture"—they are only partially erect when they stand, with their knees bent slightly, their heads tilted forward, their shoulders in a permanent shrug, and their arms floating in front of them, elbows bent, a little above their waists.

Working for any length of time with arms at table height requires a considerable expenditure of effort. The astronauts must make a conscious attempt to bend forward and force their arms down to the appropriate level, a position they would assume naturally and effortlessly on Earth. Even sitting is a problem. The body automatically assumes the semierect space neutral posture, and the crew have to use belts to keep themselves in their seats. Even then, they have to flex their abdominal muscles to keep their bodies from straightening out and popping upward.

Commonplace tasks, like getting dressed, are challenging in space. "We found it much easier to pull our legs upward to lace our shoes rather than bend down," Pogue says. "Inability to bend forward also made it harder to get the upper part of the one-piece space suits over our heads. We put our legs in from the opening in the back of the suit and then had to bend forward while we lifted the top half of the suit to get our heads through the neck ring."[33] Since Pogue's missions, NASA has made things a bit easier by redesigning the suits. They are now two-piece garments, joined by a ring at the waist.

The pace of activity during the first few hours of any mission is quite hectic, and the astronauts frequently perspire. That, too, is different in space from what it is on Earth. When the sweat emerges from the pores, it doesn't flow downward as it does under the influence of gravity. Rather it collects into pools on the surface of the skin and just sits there. The same thing happens to blood. Astronauts who've sustained minor cuts notice that the blood doesn't flow, but rather amasses into an ever-expanding globule over the wound. Also, tears behave strangely in the absence of gravity. Mike Mullane was overcome by emotion while looking down from orbit on his childhood home in New Mexico. "What happened to my tears?" he asks. "Just as with sweat and blood, tears don't flow in space. They just cling to your eyes and eyelashes."[34]

Space Sickness

About 40 percent of all astronauts experience space sickness, a continuous and sometimes debilitating nausea that lasts beyond the initial upset stomachs that in most cases disappear an hour or so after exposure to microgravity.

Even simple tasks like getting dressed or sitting down are challenging in space.

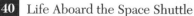

The condition is caused by mixed signals sent to the brain by the eyes and the body's balancing mechanism in the inner ear. In the absence of the constant downward pull of gravity on inner ear fluids, the eyes sense motion but the body does not. Consequently, the eyes continue to transmit up and down signals along the neural pathways to the brain. The brain, in turn, tries to match these signals up with confirming—but now nonexistent—information from the inner ear. The mismatch creates a sense of vertigo or dizziness, which makes some people nauseated.

The shuttle's medical kit contains antinausea pills. However, weightlessness is a pervasive condition in space, inside the body as well as out, so medicine taken orally tends to float around an astronaut's stomach for a long time before working its way into the intestines and being absorbed into the bloodstream. Therefore, most victims of space sickness prefer quicker-acting injections, and all astronauts are trained in the use of hypodermic syringes for this purpose. Ear patches are also available.

However, until the drug kicks in, things can get uncomfortable. It's an indelicate subject, but it happens so frequently that no accurate description of life on the shuttle would be complete without mentioning it. The astronauts have learned to take it in stride, and keep emesis (vomit) bags within easy reach during their first few days in space. For reasons that NASA's medical team has not been able to discover, this phenomenon seems confined to rookie astronauts. Those who make more than one flight rarely experience it on their subsequent missions. Spills are frequent, but crew members are good-natured about helping each other clean up the mess.

While attacks of space sickness are easy to deal with inside the shuttle, such an episode during a space walk could be fatal, as Mullane explains:

A spacesuited astronaut would have no way to get the fluid away from his face. He could aspirate [inhale] it and choke to death. Also, the emesis could clog up the oxygen circulation system and suffocate him. This is one reason why NASA never schedules a planned space walk any earlier than the third day in orbit. This allows astronauts time to get over the sickness.[35]

Other Surprises

Astronauts are well briefed on what to expect during the first hours and days of life in the weightlessness of space. Yet most of them report that the actual experiences and sensations take them by surprise. For example, it doesn't take long for the astronauts, busy as they are, to get thirsty and hungry. Their first mouthful of food or water acquaints them with another mildly unpleasant aspect of life without the stabilizing effects of gravity: to burp in space is also—often—to regurgitate. Because food and liquid weigh nothing, they don't settle to the bottom of the stomach, and an expulsion of air often brings unwanted companions with it. For this reason, the astronauts quickly develop an aversion to belching. That, however, creates another problem: the urge to pass gas is a chronic condition. Failure to do so, however, can lead to abdominal pain. For that reason, NASA discourages "gassy" food items like beans and carbonated beverages.

Many astronauts also suffer from persistent lower back pain, due to the unaccustomed muscle exertion required to keep their bodies erect (which they need to do for some of the tasks they have to perform). They also experience dry mouth and dry skin because the atmosphere in the crew compartment doesn't contain as much moisture as Earth's atmosphere does. People who spend a lot of time in air-conditioned environments sometimes experience this phenomenon on the ground; but in space there is no relief.

The senses of taste and smell seem to be less acute in space. No one is quite sure why this is so, but the continual head stuffiness that all astronauts experience is cited as a probable cause. "There seem to be some slight changes in the sense of taste, smell, appetite, and food preference," William Pogue notes.

I didn't think taste and flavors were as strong as on Earth. On our flight, we repeated taste and odor tests we had done on Earth before the flight. The results were different for each person, and no consistent patterns were determined. There does seem to be an increase in the use of condiments. Astronauts who normally avoid hot and spicy foods have been observed to use Tabasco sauce quite liberally after a few days in space.[36]

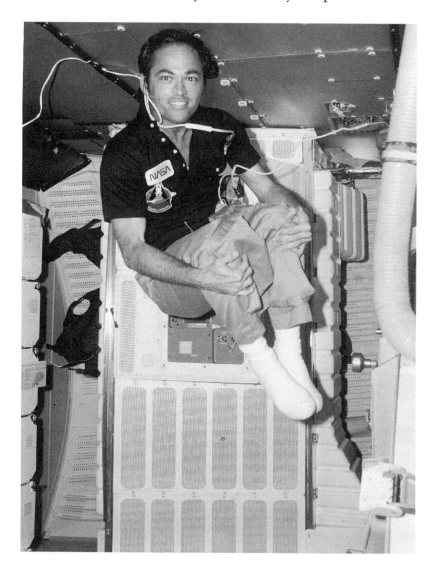

Because of the unusual muscle exertion needed to keep their bodies straight, many astronauts suffer from lower back pain. Here Robert L. Crippen does a mid-air somersault to alleviate his pain.

Another change that takes place is too subtle to be noticed by the astronauts themselves, but tests done with supersensitive voice-recognition computer interfaces indicate that their voices rise slightly in pitch. The difference, though too small for the human ear to detect, is large enough so that the devices that readily understood verbal commands on Earth have to be recalibrated to do so in space.

Lasting Effects

Almost all of the symptoms described so far vanish within days, but others linger longer. Astronauts' legs become thin and spindly and remain that way until after they return to Earth. They call the phenomenon "bird legs," and it's noticeable even on flights of very short duration. "The calves, in particular, became quite small," Pogue says. "During the first few days in space, the legs become smaller because the muscles of the legs force blood and other fluids toward the upper part of the body, thus decreasing the girth measurement of the thighs and calves. In addition, muscle tissue is progressively lost due to insufficient exercise."[37]

Shifts in body fluids also account for a related phenomenon. "The upper body swells," says Mike Mullane. "Everybody's chests—male and female—get bigger in weightlessness. When I looked at myself in the mirror, I looked as if I had been pumping iron. All the muscles in my upper body were bulging."[38] At the same time, the astronauts develop "wasp waists" because their abdominal organs, not weighed down by gravity, ride higher in their bodies than when they are on Earth. Waist measurement differentials of up to three inches have been noted.

Astronauts also grow taller in space, sometimes by as much as two inches. This happens because the vertebrae of the spine, no longer compressed by gravity, spread apart, causing the body to elongate. Unfortunately, this stretching contributes to the back pain many shuttle crew members suffer.

Many of them maintain that this chronic dull ache is the most distressing part of space travel. Pain pills, such as aspirin, are available, but the astronauts have found that the best way to get some relief is to roll themselves into a ball by pulling their knees up to their chests. They resort to this form of therapy several times a day, during breaks from their work, and say that while it doesn't eliminate the pain altogether, it does make it bearable.

Bone loss is another lasting consequence of spaceflight. As in the case of bedridden people on Earth, bones lose minerals, mainly calcium, when the body doesn't have to deal with the stress put on it by gravity. Consequently, the astronauts' bones become progressively weaker over time. The problem is not excessively debilitating on short space missions, like week-long shuttle flights, but it is a cause for concern on flights of longer duration, and NASA doctors monitor the bone loss experienced by shuttle astronauts in their

search to discover ways to lessen the effect as they prepare astronauts to work on the International Space Station and undertake a planned mission to Mars within the next twenty years. Nevertheless, the phenomenon contributes to the feeling of fatigue that many shuttle crew members report.

Two Mysteries

There are two curious effects of weightlessness that have so far baffled scientists. Almost all the astronauts report feeling excessively depressed and lethargic if they went more than three or four hours without eating. They call it "space crud." William Pogue says: "It's sort of like the down-and-out feeling you have when you're coming down with a bad cold or the flu. I still don't understand what caused this, but we learned very quickly that it was unwise to skip meals to save time. If we did,

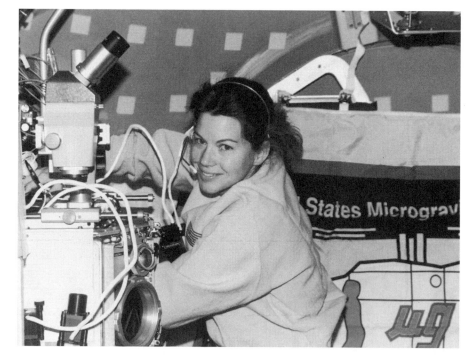

Catherine Coleman works aboard the Columbia. *Even during work times astronauts must eat every few hours to avoid feeling lethargic.*

When seven people are confined for a week or longer in a cabin the size of a small bedroom, privacy eventually becomes an issue. NASA is aware of the need for privacy and never activates the shuttle's TV cameras without first obtaining the crew's permission.

Provisions are made for each of the astronauts to have a private telephone conversation with the flight surgeon at the end of each work period, and NASA treats the information exchanged as confidential un-less it has an impact on the success of the mission.

As to constant physical proximity, the astronauts respect one another's need for quiet time alone, usually in the hour before they go to sleep. On Mike Mullane's first mission, Judy Resnick (who later lost her life in the *Challenger* explosion) was a crewmate. He says that when she needed to change her clothes, the men simply floated into the upper deck of the orbiter and left her alone in the mid-deck.

we would begin to feel bad and were much more likely to make a mistake."[39]

The second mysterious phenomenon concerns flashes of lights that astronauts appear to see when the crew compartment is darkened during sleep periods. The disturbing flashes are particularly noticeable when the shuttle is passing through one of the radiation belts that surround Earth. The leading theory is that particles of this radiation emit light waves when they are slowed down by eye fluid, but nobody has yet come up with a definitive explanation.

Although life aboard the shuttle has its inconveniences, no astronaut who has experienced it has ever expressed regret. "The best part of being in space is being weightless," insists Sally Ride, even though she experienced all the discomforts other astronauts have felt.

It feels wonderful to be able to float without effort; to slither up, down, and around the inside of the shuttle just like a seal; to be upside down as often as I'm right side up and have it make no difference. Early in my first flight I constantly felt that I was about to lose control, as though I were teetering on a balance beam or tipping over in a canoe. It's a strange, unsteady feeling that's difficult to describe, but fortunately it goes away. . . . By the third day of a week-long shuttle flight, though, all the astronauts are feeling fine. Weightlessness is pure fun, once everyone gets the hang of it.[40]

Food and Hygiene

From the point of view of astronaut comfort, no two things separate the shuttle from its spacecraft predecessors more than the kitchen and the toilet. In the midst of all the cutting-edge technology that makes the shuttle the most advanced vessel in the history of space travel, it is these relatively low-tech features that crew members single out for praise most often. Food is not only essential to health and productivity; preparing and eating it are about as close as the astronauts get to the psychologically reassuring comforts of home. And hygiene, especially when a group of people are working and living in close quarters, is crucial to morale and team spirit.

Advances in Food Preparation

The first space food was taken aloft by John Glenn in 1962, and it was limited to that which could be pureed and forced into toothpaste tube–like containers. No consideration was paid to taste. Over time freeze-dried foods were added to the menu, and the Apollo astronauts enjoyed the relative luxury of a few canned items during their trip to the moon in 1969.

With the advent of the shuttle, space food took a major leap forward. The shuttle has a fully equipped galley, or kitchen, located in the orbiter's mid-deck, close to the hatch through which astronauts enter and leave the vessel. This facility is outfitted with hot and cold water dispensers. It also has a pantry for food storage

and a convection oven—a small version of the conventional oven that is a part of most kitchen stoves—so the space travelers can heat their meals. It might seem logical for the shuttle to have a microwave oven, but NASA's engineers decided this convenient appliance might interfere with other electronic equipment.

It was also decided that a food freezer would take up too much valuable space (although freezers are carried on some missions to hold scientific experiments), so the only fresh foods the astronauts get to eat are items like nuts, which don't degrade at room temperature. Also, although the oven is prized by the astronauts because it enables them to enjoy hot meals, they cannot actually use it to roast or bake. It does nothing more than heat precooked food.

Meals are eaten from individual trays, which have compartments to hold the various food containers to keep them from floating around the cabin. The astronauts attach these trays to their laps by means of Velcro strips, and each of them has a set of ordinary dining utensils, including a knife, fork, large and small spoons, scissors, and even a can opener. "But," says Bill Nelson,

> like many campers, by the second day I had stowed the knife and fork. For the rest of the flight, I ate everything, including my main courses, with my spoon. . . . The spoon was not only easier to clean but easier to eat with, because the food remained stuck to the surface by its own moisture.

With the knife and fork, morsels would float away and I would have to go after them.[41]

Nutrition and Taste

Foods are preserved by a variety of methods. Some are dehydrated or freeze-dried, requiring only the addition of water to restore them to their natural condition. Other items, such as meat and poultry, are packed with juices or gravy in foil pouches. Prior to the flight, these are cooked to destroy bacteria. When it's time to eat them, all the astronauts have to do is reheat them in the oven. Other foods are irradiated to kill potentially harmful microbes, and others, like candy bars, require no special treatment and are carried aboard the shuttle in the same wrapping they have on Earth.

"I was particularly impressed by the packaging for the food," says Nelson.

> The rehydratable items were sealed in square, nestable containers designed to maximize storage space. Each individual package, such as sweet-and-sour chicken, had been precooked and all the water removed. Then it had been sealed in a small, rigid plastic bowl with a flexible, see-through film lid. Mealtime preparation was simple: Water was introduced into the package without breaking the seal through a hollow needle inserted in the base of the cup. After the water had been mixed with the food and the food had been reconstituted, it could be heated. . . . When it was ready, all you had to do was remove the package lid with a knife or scissors and eat with conventional utensils.[42]

NASA employs a staff of nutritionists who help the astronauts plan menus that will not only please their palates, but also ensure that they get the proper amounts of vitamins, min-

A Typical Shuttle Menu

Here, from NASA's *Space Food and Nutrition Educator's Guide*, is a typical three-day menu that a shuttle astronaut might choose:

"**Day One**
Breakfast: dried peaches, cornflakes, orange-pineapple drink, cocoa
Lunch: ham, cheese spread, two tortillas, pineapple, cashews, strawberry drink
Dinner: chicken à la king, cauliflower with cheese, brownie, grape drink

Day Two
Breakfast: dried pears, beef patties, scrambled eggs, orange juice
Lunch: peanut butter, apple jelly, two tortillas, fruit cocktail, trail mix, peach-apricot drink
Dinner: frankfurters, macaroni and cheese, green beans with mushrooms, tropical punch

Day Three
Breakfast: dried apricots, breakfast roll, chocolate instant drink, grapefruit drink
Lunch: turkey salad spread, two tortillas, peaches, granola bar, lemonade
Dinner: spaghetti with meat sauce, Italian vegetables, butterscotch pudding, orange drink"

erals, proteins, and carbohydrates to keep them healthy and energetic during their mission. The general guidelines are 1,600 to 2,000 calories of carbohydrates, 400 to 600 calories of protein, and 600 to 1,000 calories of fat.

"I had expected [space food] to be bland," Nelson says.

Instead, it was quite tasty. Many of the foods were actually available on grocery store shelves. Seventy-two different food items were available, ranging from beef Stroganoff with noodles, to Mexican scrambled eggs, to shrimp cocktail. The dietitian told me I was allowed to design my own menu so I would not have to eat foods I did not ordinarily like. Each crew member would be supplied with three balanced meals a day . . . with all the recommended dietary allowances of vitamins and minerals necessary to perform in the environment of space.[43]

Come and Get It

When the astronauts have chosen their menus, the food is assembled in containers labeled with colored dots so it will be easy for them to find their own meals when they are in orbit. General food items—including snacks like candies, cookies, and nuts—are available for anyone to eat any time they feel hungry and to keep their energy levels up between meals. Salt and pepper are also provided, but in a form different from how they are found on Earth. If a granulated substance, like salt or pepper, were shaken in weightlessness, it would fly off and get drawn into the air filters. So the shuttle galley is stocked with salt and pepper water in small, squeezable containers, much like eyedrop bottles. To use them, an astronaut puts the nozzle against the food he or she wants to season and forces out a few drops, which adhere to the surface of the food.

Astronauts take turns preparing meals. "Usually one or two astronauts make a meal for the whole crew," says Sally Ride, who provides a description of getting a typical lunch ready.

Open the food locker and see what has been planned for lunch. How about hot dogs, macaroni and cheese, peanuts and

Meals are eaten from trays with separate compartments. Packages are labeled with colored dots so astronauts can find their own food items.

lemonade? Get out the food trays. . . . Attach the trays to the wall with Velcro so they won't float away. Put one package of peanuts in each food tray. Turn on the oven, open the oven door, and slide in the hot dogs in their sealed foil bags. Fit the cartons of dehydrated macaroni and cheese, one at a time, into the water dispenser. Squeeze each macaroni carton to mix in the water, then place it in the oven, too. Use the water dispenser to add water to each plastic carton of powered lemonade. Slide a straw into each carton and put one lemonade carton in each tray. Remove the hot food from the oven and put a carton of macaroni and cheese and a pouch of hot dogs in each tray. Get out the bread, butter, catsup, and mustard. Crew members have to make their own hot dog sandwiches; once a sandwich is made, it can't be put down because it would float apart. Call the rest of the crew to "come and get it." We gather on the mid-deck to enjoy meals together like a family. The engineers at Mission Control try not to call us while we're eating, so we have some time to talk to one another and relax. But we don't look like a family sitting down to lunch on Earth. We don't eat at a table; our tables are the trays strapped to our legs. We don't sit in chairs. Each of us finds a comfortable spot—maybe floating near the ceiling, or upside down in the middle of the cabin.[44]

Unexpected Difficulties

Ride points out that some astronauts eat upside down, raising the question: how is it possible to swallow food in space? Upside down or right side up, in the absence of gravity, how does food flow along the esophagus into the stomach? In fact, there is no difficulty swallowing either solids or liquids in microgravity. In swallowing, the substance is forced along the esophagus by a series of muscular contractions; gravity does not play a role on Earth or in space.

Some foods, prepared as a matter of course on Earth, require planning in space, as Ride explains:

> A peanut butter sandwich is simple to fix on Earth. But in space it takes two astronauts to prepare one. The first time I tried to make a peanut butter sandwich, I held the jar of peanut butter, unscrewed the top, and found I needed another hand. If I let go of either the lid or the jar, it would float away. So I tossed the lid to another astronaut and picked up a knife—but with the jar in one hand and the knife in the other, I had no way to reach for the bread! After that, I asked someone else to hold the bread or the jar whenever I wanted a sandwich.[45]

Crumbs can be a problem because they tend to clog up the shuttle's air filters. That's why NASA dietitians encourage the use of tortillas rather than bread. The astronauts also find tortillas easier to manipulate than

Astronauts' Top Ten Food Choices

A few years ago, dietitians at the Johnson Space Center in Houston, Texas, analyzed menus selected by shuttle astronauts up to that point and discovered that the following foods were the favorites. The percentages, published on NASA's Neurolab web page, indicate how many of the space travelers chose the item at least once.

1. butter cookies—87%
2. dried beef—82%
3. granola bars—80%
4. cashew nuts—77%
5. macadamia nuts—77%
6. trail mix—73%
7. shrimp cocktail—69%
8. potatoes au gratin—69%
9. chocolate pudding—69%
10. almonds—69%

Since swallowing is not affected by microgravity, eating upside down (as shown here) or right side up makes no difference in space.

slices of bread; rolling up a tortilla is a one-person job, whereas—as Sally Ride discovered—making a sandwich from two slices of bread requires assistance.

The tortilla technique made it possible for Bill Nelson to enjoy a steak.

Trying to eat [a steak] in zero gravity presented a messy problem—keeping the steak juice from floating away when the steak was pulled out of its plastic container. Franklin [Diaz], the first Hispanic-American astronaut, solved this problem for us with a package of tortillas he had

brought along. He just wrapped the steak and its juices in the tortilla. It could then be eaten as easily as a steak sandwich without any mess.[46]

Think Before Drinking

Astronauts must use a straw to drink because of the unusual behavior of water in microgravity. In a weightless environment, all liquids will float around aimlessly if they are not kept tightly sealed in containers. Even if water could be poured into a normal, lidless drinking glass, it would creep up the sides of the interior surface, ooze over the edge, and creep down the exterior surface. This phenomenon is caused by the attractive force that exists between the molecules of the liquid and those of the container. Water molecules that aren't attached to a surface in this way accumulate into spheres, which float freely around the cabin.

Bill Nelson encountered this problem while trying to eat a grapefruit he had carried into space to pay tribute to the economic importance of the citrus industry in his native state of Florida.

I peeled the grapefruit in its entirety and then pried apart the segments into manageable pieces. However, the first time I tried to open one of the segments, the juice squirted out, formed a ball, and floated off. I tried to go after it with my fingers, but the moment I touched it, it broke into countless little droplets. I was obliged to spend a while floating around the cabin with my mouth open, inhaling grapefruit juice globules.[47]

The shuttle doesn't carry carbonated beverages because they contribute to flatulence and they're too bulky to store. Also, alcohol is forbidden—even for Russian cosmonauts, who were permitted a daily ration of vodka on the Mir Space Station. But that doesn't stop the astronauts from having fun at mealtimes, as Sally Ride recalls:

On one of my flights, we set a cookie floating in the middle of the room and then "flew" an astronaut, with his mouth

An astronaut attempts to catch a floating Girl Scout cookie.

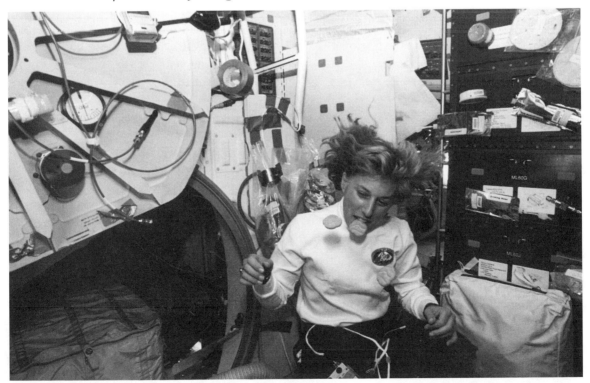

wide open, across the cabin to capture it. We often share bags of peanuts because it gives us an excuse to play catch, floating peanuts back and forth into each other's mouths. We race to capture spinning bananas and carrots and practice catching spoonfuls of food in our mouths while they twirl in midair.[48]

Cleaning up after meals—or food games—is an important activity for the maintenance of safety aboard the shuttle. Empty containers, and even tiny particles of food, could get sucked into air filters or damage delicate equipment. Just as they take turns preparing meals, the astronauts share cleaning duties. Reusable utensils are wiped down with moistened germicidal cloths and stowed away. Nonreusable leftovers are collected in trash bags and stored in a compartment beneath the floor of the mid-deck. All garbage is brought back to Earth; if it was disposed of in space, it would instantly freeze and pose a hazard to satellites and other manned missions.

Waste Management

Dealing with human waste has been a problem for the manned space program from its inception. The first astronauts, those involved in Project Mercury in the early 1960s, had to urinate into collection bags sewn into their space suits. No provision was made for defecation other than to feed them a low-fiber diet for several days before their flights. Since none of those flights lasted more than thirty-four hours, this precaution was considered adequate. For Project Gemini, during which flights lasted up to fourteen days, the astronauts had to use a clear plastic bag, which came to be known as the Gemini Bag. They affixed it to their buttocks with adhesive strips and sealed it immediately

after use. Usually—but not always—they were quick enough to prevent the bag's contents from escaping. Even today Gemini Bags are carried aboard the shuttle, but for emergency use only. Still, says astronaut Ron Evans: "There ain't no graceful way."[49]

The shuttle toilet is a major advance over this primitive method of waste disposal. The Waste Collection System, as it is called in NASA parlance, can be used with equal ease by both men and women, although the astronauts admit it still presents serious challenges. It also lacks the privacy that Earth bathroom facilities provide. It's located in the orbiter's mid-deck—right next to the galley—and the astronaut using it is separated from his or her crewmates only by a curtain.

Since the astronauts cannot remain in a sitting position in the absence of gravity, they must clamp themselves to the toilet's seat. "On each side of the toilet are things that look like handles," says Mike Mullane. "Prior to solid waste elimination, an astronaut floats over the seat, pulls up on these handles, and twists them inward over the thighs. [A] spring force clamps the thighs and keeps the astronaut from floating away."[50]

Because water doesn't flow in space, the shuttle toilet uses air to deal with waste material. There's a small opening, four inches in diameter, in the middle of the seat. A flat, retractable cover sits over the opening when the toilet is not in use. Just below this cover, the seat is perforated with a ring of tiny suction devices. A silver-knobbed lever to the right of the toilet causes the cover to retract and activates the suction function. Cabin air is sucked into the toilet and carries solid waste to the bottom of the bowl, where it is collected in a bag made from a material that allows the suctioned air to pass through while trapping everything else. When the astronaut is done, he or she removes this bag, seals it, and stores it with the rest of the garbage to be returned to Earth.

Learning the Basics

One of the strangest aspects of astronaut training is learning how to use the shuttle's toilet. "The small size of the toilet opening makes aim critical to the success of the operation," Mullane explains.

Recognizing this, NASA engineers have built a toilet trainer at the Johnson Space Center with which astronauts practice their aim. This trainer consists of an upward pointing television camera set in the toilet bowl. Astronauts sit on this toilet and check their aim by viewing a television that sits in front of the trainer. When they have properly positioned their bodies, they memorize the position of their thighs and buttocks in relation to the toilet seat. To say this training takes a lot of the glamour out of being an astronaut is an obvious understatement.[51]

Urination makes fewer technical demands. The shuttle urinal consists of a hose attached to the front of the toilet. Urine is sucked through the hose into a holding tank. When the tank is full, it is emptied into space. Unlike solid waste, which would freeze into objects large enough to damage spacecraft,

Even in space astronauts must attend to housekeeping duties, including cleaning toilets.

urine freezes into minute, harmless crystals.

To accommodate the anatomical differences between men and women, the shuttle urination device has a removable cone-shaped cup that attaches to the end of the hose for use by female astronauts. "Each astronaut has a personal cup that fits onto the tube," says Sally Ride. "To use the urine cup, I hold it next to my body while floating in the bathroom, and then—a very important step—I turn on the air suction that flows through the flexible hose. The air suction replaces gravity and pulls the urine down the tube and into the waste tank."[52]

The shuttle toilet makes life in space a lot easier on the astronauts, but it isn't perfect. In fact, it has failed on several missions, forcing the crew to revert to earlier waste management procedures. Each shuttle crew member is provided with two solid waste collection bags per day in case such an emergency arises. In these circumstances, they wear adult diapers for urine collection.

Coming Clean

Each astronaut carries a personal hygiene kit into space. It includes items such as toothbrushes, dental floss, nail clippers, deodorant, a comb and hairbrush, and lip balm and skin lotion (dry lips and skin are frequently reported problems in the orbiter's drier-than-Earth atmosphere). Men also have shaving cream and a razor, or an electric razor if they prefer, and women have feminine hygiene products and they can bring cosmetics with them if they wish. There's no shower on the shuttle, but a personal hygiene station, lo-

Although a shuttle does not have a shower, there is a personal hygiene station where astronauts can shave or wash themselves.

Astronauts wash their hair with a special shampoo that does not require rinsing.

cated near the galley and toilet, allows the crew members to wash themselves. It has a mirror and a water dispenser. Each member of the crew is assigned one washcloth and one towel for each day their mission will last.

"On the space plane we don't have a sink, bathtub or shower because water coming out of a faucet would float in little blobs all over the cabin," says Sally Ride.

Instead, we have a water gun, a hose with a trigger control on the nozzle. I put a washcloth next to the nozzle and wet it; then I use it with soap to wash my hands and face. . . . The toothbrush I use looks ordinary, but it has a special digestible toothpaste already in the bristles. I have to swallow the toothpaste because I can't spit it into a sink (remember, there is no sink). Every morning, I unwrap a new toothbrush, use it, swallow the toothpaste, and throw the brush away. I brush and comb my hair just as I would on Earth, but it doesn't do much good; my weightless hair still floats around my head.[53]

The astronauts use a special shampoo that requires no rinsing. They massage it into their hair, being careful not to create any floating bubbles, then remove it with a towel. Shaving does not create a problem for the shuttle's air filters because hair bristles either adhere to the lathered razor or are sucked into the electric shaver.

International Cooperation on the Shuttle

"NASA and Foreign-Born Astronauts," a report published by the American Immigration Law Foundation, makes the point that although the human exploration of space began as a hostile competition between the United States and the Soviet Union in the late 1950s and early 1960s, when the two superpowers were threatening each other with nuclear weapons, it has, during the years since the shuttle was first launched, become instead an opportunity to promote harmony among the countries of the world.

"While the early race into space during the 1950s and 1960s was a Cold War–driven event, today's space program is one of international cooperation," the 1990 report says. "Almost every U.S. space shuttle mission includes at least one foreign-born crew member who provides critical expertise to the team. And as construction continues on the International Space Station, the future promises to show that in space, everyone is an immigrant."

As of late 2001, astronauts from the following countries have flown on the shuttle: Argentina, Brazil, Canada, France, Germany, India, Italy, Japan, Morocco, Spain, Sweden, Switzerland, and Russia.

The International Space Station is open to astronauts from all countries.

Wet garbage, including uneaten food, is stowed in plastic bags—along with solid body waste—beneath the floor of the mid-deck. The shuttle's air-conditioning system is efficient enough to remove any odor emanating from what is in effect an orbiting garbage dump. Dry waste, mostly paper, is collected in canvas bags attached by Velcro to the orbiter's walls. For long missions, and those where the tasks are expected to generate a lot of waste paper, a trash compactor is available. But it's infrequently carried because it takes up space that would otherwise be devoted to storing the crew's gear.

Each astronaut gets one change of underwear per day in space, along with a couple of extra shirts and shorts. Dirty laundry is stored in a clothes hamper—a canvas bag that's usually tucked away in the air lock to keep it out of everyone's way. It's the responsibility of every astronaut to keep the crew compartment clean. Debris is gathered up quickly, both for safety reasons and because living in a cluttered or dirty environment would dampen crew morale.

Although the shuttle has made life in space much easier than it was for astronauts who went aloft in earlier vessels, the absence of gravity makes it impossible to re-create conditions exactly as they are on Earth. Significant inconveniences remain, but the crew members accept this as part of the pioneering nature of space travel. The hardships they have to endure, and the ingenuity they employ to overcome them, are part of the challenge they were seeking when they chose to join NASA and become explorers of the frontier that space represents.

5 Working

Space shuttle missions are carefully scripted to minimize waste of time. Every minute of the astronauts' day is minutely planned, and each of them carries a clipboard on which they check off their duties as they perform them. Back on the ground, mission control monitors their activities, chiding them—gently—if they begin to fall behind schedule, and offering helpful suggestions to deal with unforeseen situations. Much of the work deals with scientific experiments, both for NASA and for university researchers and private corporations. If the experiments are too complicated to carry out inside the orbiter, a special module, called Spacelab, can be carried in the cargo bay instead of some other payload. The astronauts get in and out of Spacelab through the air lock, which they also use when they have to do space walks. The air lock is connected to Spacelab by a tube through which the crew members float.

Special Tools

Although objects, being weightless, are easy to lift and maneuver in space, working on the shuttle challenges the astronauts with a unique set of problems. On Earth, for example, turning a screw is a routine activity because gravity keeps the worker securely fixed to the ground. In space, however, when an astronaut exerts a twisting force on the handle of a screwdriver, he or she is as likely to turn as the screw is. To overcome difficulties such as these, there are numerous foot restraints bolted to the floor of the shuttle that enable the crew members to anchor themselves.

NASA engineers have also invented special tools to make work on the shuttle less physically demanding and time-consuming. These include a zero-reaction power tool, which through an intricate arrangement of gears and springs allows an astronaut to multiply the force of certain hand motions by a factor of ten thousand. A spring-driven hammer permits a space worker to staple objects together without propelling himself across the cabin. Velcro and other adhesive strips placed at strategic locations let the astronauts keep their tools from floating away, and lights attached to headgear keep out-of-the way areas well illuminated while leaving hands free.

Making notes, and other tasks that require writing, is also more difficult in space than it is on the ground, where gravity pulls ink down toward the tip of a pen. For this reason, the ink cartridges in the pens that astronauts use are gas pressurized. They also use retractable pencils and felt-tipped pens to write. Reading instructional manuals while working is difficult because a book left unattended will float away. Even if the covers of the book can be attached to a surface by Velcro, the pages tend to fan out if they are not held down. Astronauts struggled with this problem for years before NASA provided them with laptop computers that can display both text and graphics. They attach the computers near their workstations with Velcro

In the weightlessness of space, many tasks take ten times longer than they do on the ground.

and scroll through the material with a touch of a finger.

Despite these aids, astronauts estimate that many tasks, even very simple ones, take ten times longer to do in the weightlessness of space than they do on the ground. The unusual physical demands and the frustration at the amount of time required to do tasks that would be effortless on Earth contribute to an ongoing sense of tiredness that most crew members report having to struggle with during their flights. Adding to their fatigue is the stress caused by the knowledge that one mistake could jeopardize a $400 million mission, or—far worse—put their crewmates' lives at risk.

Communication

Good communication, both among the astronauts on the shuttle and between the shuttle and mission control, is vital to the success of

In-Flight Emergencies

The shuttle is equipped with smoke detectors and fire extinguishers, located near electrical devices that could possibly overheat. It also has an emergency oxygen supply. Should the cabin suddenly depressurize, all vents automatically seal and enough oxygen is pumped in to enable the astronauts to breathe and to bring the pressure back up to acceptable levels.

There are provisions for an in-flight rescue, but success would depend on how quickly another shuttle could be sent into orbit. Even then, transferring astronauts from the disabled vessel is a complicated and untested procedure.

Each orbiter carries two thirty-inch spherical Personal Rescue Enclosures. One astronaut, wearing a pressure suit, climbs inside while another zippers the enclosure around him or her. A third and fourth astronaut, protected by extravehicular activity (EVA) suits, then transfer the enclosure through the air lock to the air lock of the rescue ship, which is orbiting nearby. The process is repeated until the only astronauts left are those wearing the EVA gear, and they have to get themselves safely into the functioning orbiter's air lock.

any space mission. To facilitate this, the crew members often wear lightweight headsets, consisting of an earphone, which clips on their ear, with a microphone attached to it by a thin, rigid cable. The device is connected to a control unit that the astronaut attaches to his or her clothes by means of Velcro. A switch on this unit allows voice communication either with the shuttle's onboard intercom or with mission control. Although the cabin is small, the hum of the air conditioner and other life-support equipment sometimes makes it diffi-

cult for the astronauts to hear one another clearly if they are more than a few feet apart.

The shuttle has a fax machine to exchange written communications with mission control, and the onboard computers can receive data directly from computers on the ground. Also, television cameras transmit pictures of the crew at work to their Earth-bound helpers.

In the early days of spaceflight, communication between mission control and astronauts in orbit was limited to times when the orbiting vehicle was within range of a ground station. Rarely was that for more than five minutes at a time. Now, thanks to communication satellites, the shuttle and the mission controllers are at each other's beck and call twenty-four hours a day, even though the messages must travel a roundabout way.

"Even when the shuttle is on the opposite side of the Earth from Houston, the crew remains in contact through a network of geosynchronous communication satellites called tracking, data, and relay satellites (TDRS)," says Mike Mullane.

When a crew member presses the microphone button and calls Mission Control, the signal doesn't go directly to the ground. It is transmitted to whatever TDRS is in view (there are three). This satellite then relays it to the TDRS system ground station at White Sands, New Mexico. Here it is electronically processed and retransmitted to another geosync satellite (different from the TDRS) which, in turn, relays it to Mission Control in Houston, Texas. Even at the speed of light (about 186,000 miles per second), the distance and processing time involved in this relay are great enough to cause a several-second delay in the communication. In fact, by the time the shuttle data appears on mission control's computer screens it's about six seconds old. Mission Control's transmissions to the crew follow the same communication path in reverse.[54]

Housework

Routine maintenance and housekeeping activities are shared among all members of the crew. And there's plenty to do. Dr. Roberta Bondar, a Canadian astronaut who conducted scientific experiments during one shuttle mission, recalls that the astronauts quickly learn that

when they're not working—they're working. Often 18 hours a day. Just keeping

the orbiter clean and operational is a continuous task. There are air filters to clean and change. There is food to prepare. There is trash to stow. The extra water produced by the fuel cells has to be pumped out the back of the shuttle. And of course there are always reports to send to the ground crew.[55]

Many of the chores are similar to those done on Earth: dusting, vacuuming, changing lightbulbs. The walls have to be scrubbed frequently to remove particles of food and liquid and even—sometimes—the residue left by a space-sick astronaut. But because they are conducted in space, these everyday tasks require a very un-Earth-like degree of cooperation.

Doing Public Relations for NASA

As busy as the astronauts are during a shuttle mission, NASA insists they take time to do public relations work while in orbit. The space agency realizes that its future depends on taxpayer support and makes the crew available for TV and other media interviews via the satellite communications network that links the shuttle with mission control.

The space program must compete for funding with other government agencies, and its administrators are aware that members of Congress are more likely to approve budget requests if their constituents feel well disposed toward manned spaceflight. So astronauts become goodwill ambassadors in between their many other duties, putting a human face on what would otherwise be a dry and technical subject.

For example, in July 2001 CBS TV news reporter Melissa McDermott interviewed the crew of *Atlantis* during a mission to the International Space Station. What fol-

lows, excerpted from a CBS transcript, is an exchange with first-time astronaut Charles Hobaugh.

"McDermott: You're the rookie up there. . . . Tell us what it was like the first time you realized you are actually up in space.

Hobaugh: It was like living a dream. It was like it wasn't happening at all. . . . We got that light, floating feeling that is really strange seeing everybody float around and doing things. That feeling almost made you feel that everything was in slow motion.

McDermott: Are there any fears or anything in the back of your mind that you're thinking 'I hope this doesn't happen'?

Hobaugh: Not at all. It was the most pleasurable experience I've ever had and there was never any downside to it or never any fear. . . . We had a great time from the time we began training until this moment and I am sure it will continue from here."

Bondar recalls one occasion when it took three astronauts to close a drawer containing plant experiments she was working on. She pushed against the ceiling with her hands so her feet would press the lid closed, while two of her crewmates fastened the clasps and pushed the closed drawer into its slot in a cabinet.

All the astronauts are trained in photography, and one is usually assigned to make a photographic (or videographic) record of the others at work. They also film Earth, both for personal mementos and for scientific reasons. Photography from the shuttle has played an important role in tracking hurricanes and other weather patterns, charting soil erosion, and recording the encroachment of civilization on rain forests.

Rendezvous in Space

One of the most dramatic jobs the shuttle is called upon to perform is docking with another space vehicle. When the Russian space station Mir was still in orbit, the shuttle linked up with it several times to deliver and retrieve American astronauts who spent time on the foreign vessel studying the long-term effects of microgravity on the human body. Now the shuttle routinely docks with the International Space Station, both transporting astronauts and delivering components. Docking procedures, or rendezvous, are carried out by the commander and the pilot of the shuttle; the mission specialists are just spectators.

An astronaut moves toward the shuttle window to photograph Earth.

A pilot moves through the tunnel connecting his spacecraft with the International Space Station.

To dock, the commander and pilot use the shuttle's reaction control engines, a series of small rocket engines located between the nose and cockpit of the orbiter. These engines point in different directions, and firing them in various combinations provides total control over the shuttle's movements—up and down, right and left—and the vessel's speed. Considering that both the shuttle and the craft it is trying to link up with are traveling at about 17,500 miles an hour and that the docking ports, which have to merge precisely, are only a few feet in diameter, there is little margin for error.

First, the shuttle commander uses the re-action control engines to bring the craft into orbit behind the target vehicle. Then, he slowly draws it closer, while lining up the docking ports. To accomplish this, he may have to fire the engines for brief bursts hundreds of times. Until the two spacecraft are within two miles of each other, he keeps track of the other vessel's position with the shuttle's radar system; from the two-mile mark on, his eyes take over. Finally, when the two spacecraft are properly aligned, he slowly reduces the shuttle's speed to almost zero (relative to the other craft—they're both still traveling at an orbital velocity of roughly 17,500 miles an hour) and engages six titanium hooks in the docking ports, turning the two vessels into one.

Strangely, in order to close the distance between the shuttle and the vehicle it is chasing, the commander has to reduce—not increase—

Astronauts are often required to deploy or retrieve satellites from orbit.

its speed. When the speed of an orbiting space vehicle increases, its orbit also increases in altitude. The laws of the physics of motion dictate that the higher the orbit, the slower the vessel travels. Therefore, to narrow the distance between two orbiting spacecraft, the one following must slow down to decrease the altitude of its orbit and, thus, increase its speed. This slowing is accomplished by firing the braking rocket engines. After a series of such firings, the distance will close to zero and the vehicles will dock.

Launching Satellites

The placing of satellites into orbit is another task astronauts are required to perform on many shuttle flights. Mission specialists use the shuttle Remote Manipulator System (RMS) to deploy and retrieve satellites from orbit and to add components to the International Space Station. The RMS is a fifty-foot robotic arm that transfers objects to and from the cargo bay. The mission specialists control it from computers located at a workstation in the rear of the cockpit. Windows allow them to see into the cargo bay and a television camera on the arm gives them a close-up view of the work in progress. Like a human arm, the RMS has three joints—shoulder, elbow, and wrist—each of which has a full range of motion. A grappling device on the end enables the astronaut at the controls to attach it to satellites in the cargo bay.

Usually, two mission specialists are assigned primary responsibility for operating the RMS, but deploying a satellite is a team effort. "It is not an easy job to launch a satellite," says Sally Ride, who specialized in using the robotic arm.

Before a flight, astronauts practice every step over and over so that they will be able to release the satellite at exactly the right time, at exactly the right spot over the Earth, and with the shuttle pointing in exactly the right direction. During the countdown to the satellite launch, the crew works as a team—a very well-trained team working very closely together. Each astronaut "plays a position" on the flight deck: two are seated (wearing seat belts to avoid floating away from the computers at a critical moment), one is near the windows, and one is floating behind the seats near the satellite switches.[56]

Tension is high during the deployment of a satellite, which may be worth several hundred million dollars and may have taken engineers years to build. "Can you imagine lifting a satellite from the shuttle payload bay that's the size of two Greyhound buses . . . and is fragile as an egg?" asks Mike Mullane. "To compound the difficulty of the job, imagine having only inches of clearance between the satellite and the shuttle structure."[57]

Space Science

Space offers a unique opportunity to conduct scientific experiments in the absence of gravity and in a near-perfect vacuum, two conditions that are impossible to achieve on Earth. Mission specialists carry out research on the

Many astronauts conduct tests on themselves as part of their research. Here, a mission specialist performs a Pulmonary Function Test (PFT).

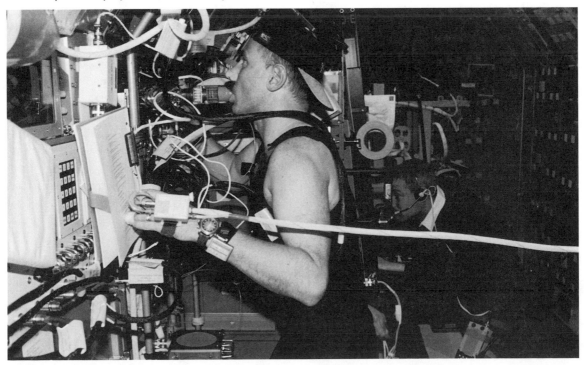

shuttle, in the hope of discovering applications that will improve industrial and laboratory procedures on Earth. But they are also preparing the way for the day when we will be able to construct manufacturing plants in space. Studies indicate that this will lead to great advances in pharmaceuticals, metallurgy, and biochemistry. Observations from the shuttle have also helped in the fields of Earth science, physics, and astronomy. Finally, tests done on the astronauts themselves pave the way for long-duration space travel.

"What kind of scientific experiments do we conduct in space?" asks Sally Ride.

We observe the stars and the Earth from our position two hundred miles up. On some flights we carry telescopes outside in the cargo bay. Because our orbit is above the atmosphere, these telescopes get a clearer view of the sun, stars, planets, and galaxies than any telescope on Earth. . . . Information gathered at shuttle height can help scientists study storms, air pollution, and volcanic eruptions and learn more about the planet we live on.[58]

The mission specialists involved in scientific experiments investigate ways to manufacture new substances—especially medicines, metals, or crystals. They also use themselves as guinea pigs, and record data about how their bodies function to help medical researchers learn about the effects of weightlessness in preparation for longer space voyages in the future.

Each shuttle mission has more than one objective. On Bill Nelson's mission, the astronauts were required to launch a telecommunications satellite, measure ultraviolet radiation bombarding Earth from space, and observe Halley's comet. In addition, he had to perform ten different biomedical experiments, including one to study the effects of weight-

lessness on the inner ear mechanism the body uses to maintain balance. "It required me to stand in a swing-like structure with sensors attached to my cheeks and a blackout hood over my head," he recalls.

The sensors measured the movement of my eyes. When the structure swung gently to and fro in about a twenty-degree arc, I was asked to keep my eyes fixed on an imaginary boat sailing on the horizon. These data were added to data already recorded by NASA doctors. The hope is that, in the near future, either an apparatus can be built to pre-adapt astronauts to zero gravity, or drugs can be developed that will . . . alleviate all travel sickness.[59]

Spacelab

While many scientific experiments, like the ones Bill Nelson participated in, are conducted inside the orbiter, some require the addition of Spacelab, the module that turns the shuttle's cargo bay into an orbiting laboratory. For Dr. Roberta Bondar's flight, Spacelab contained experiments for the first International Microgravity Laboratory, a collaborative effort involving scientists from many countries around the world. In addition to the lab itself, the shuttle carried an unusual cargo consisting of oat and wheat seeds, hamsters, mice, frogs, and crystals to study how both living and inorganic matter behaved when the force of Earth's gravity on them was negated.

For eight days Bondar and two other mission specialists glided through the tube connecting the orbiter to Spacelab so they could conduct their experiments. "For the crew, one of the fun things about this flight is floating to work through the tunnel and coming up into a bright, humming laboratory," she says. "In order to conduct the many experiments planned for this one mission, Spacelab's limited room is packed with banks of sophisticated equipment running from floor to ceiling."[60]

Concentration on the part of the mission specialists is of paramount importance. They follow a minute-by-minute work schedule and are in constant communication with scientists at mission control. "The crew must handle potentially hazardous chemicals and hypodermic needles," Bondar says.

They must use different kinds of cameras and videotape recorders to carefully record the scientific data. They must relay long, detailed mathematical readings to the ground crews. Because space inside the lab is so limited, critical pieces of the equipment, such as the microscope, must be assembled each time they are used and then taken apart. Lights must be set up for photographs; seeds must be planted; loose, floating cables must be restrained; experimental containers must be moved from one compartment to another.[61]

Because there is so much to do each day, every task is listed on an overall daily plan called the Payload Crew Activity Plan (PCAP). "For each activity on the PCAP, there is also a detailed check list to lead the astronauts through it," Bondar says. "The PCAP guides each astronaut through every minute of every hour of every day of the mission. And when the gang on the ground want to change something, a new slice of the Payload Crew Activity Plan is beamed up to the orbiter via satellite."[62]

Working in space is in some respects easier than it is on Earth, and in some respects harder. Weightlessness can be both friend and

The Payload Assist Module

The shuttle's maximum orbiting altitude is six hundred miles. When mission specialists launch communications satellites, which orbit at twenty-two thousand miles, they use a device called the Payload Assist Module (PAM).

Before the shuttle lifts off, the PAM, which has a small rocket motor, is joined to the satellite and both are placed on a giant turntable in the cargo bay. Once the shuttle reaches orbit and the cargo bay doors are opened, the turntable spins the satellite and the attached PAM to balance any unevenness in the rocket's thrust. Then springs push the satellite off the turntable and out of the cargo bay. When it is far enough away so the shuttle won't be damaged, the rocket ignites and burns until the satellite reaches the appropriate altitude. When the satellite is in orbit, the PAM separates, falls toward Earth, and eventually burns up in the atmosphere.

The PAM can lift satellites weighing up to 4,160 pounds. The procedure is conducted by two astronauts working at computer terminals at the workstation in the back of the orbiter's cockpit.

foe when it comes to performing the tasks that the astronauts are called upon to do. Most of the crew find their work to be rewarding, but they also say that much of it is repetitive, perhaps because they've practiced each aspect of it so often during their training. All of them are buoyed by the knowledge that what they are doing is helping to expand the limits of science and that what they accomplish will one day improve the quality of life back on Earth.

Space Walks

Walking and working outside the shuttle are the most challenging and risky activities astronauts perform while in space. For up to seven hours, as they orbit Earth at almost eighteen thousand miles per hour, their lives depend on a suit that must function as a one-person spacecraft, providing all the protection that the shuttle itself does. Though the danger is great, no catastrophes have yet occurred, and space walks (or extravehicular activities [EVAs], as they are called by NASA) have been the occasion of the manned space program's most towering achievements.

The Space Suit

The first space walk took place on March 2, 1965. Russian cosmonaut Alexi Leonov spent just twenty-four minutes outside of a spacecraft called *Voskhod 2*, and he almost didn't make it back alive. A failure of the air-pressure system inside his space suit made it swell like a balloon, causing him to get stuck in the hatch when he was trying to return to his vessel. After a lengthy struggle, he somehow managed to wriggle through the narrow porthole. Astronaut Ed White—the first American spacewalker, who ventured outside the *Gemini 4* space capsule three months after Leonov's near disaster—also experienced problems with his suit: the temperature controls failed and he had to return after just twenty minutes outside the capsule.

Since those first tentative steps, the art and science of space suit design has come a long way. Drawing on fields as different as deep-sea diving, medieval armor, and stretch underwear, NASA's engineers have created a suit that has performed flawlessly on dozens of missions. They spent more than $167 million to come up with what they call the Extravehicular Mobility Unit (EMU). "Shuttle suits are assembled from modular [interchangeable] parts manufactured in various sizes of torso, a variety of sleeve lengths and lower torso sizes, and a 'one size fits all' helmet," says space historian Lillian Kozloski. "The suit can be broken down following each mission so parts can be cleaned, dried, and then reused by other astronauts on subsequent missions. Since 1985, only gloves have been custom-fitted to each astronaut to relieve hand fatigue, carrying a price tag of $20,000 apiece."[63]

Each 275-pound, $1 million suit is composed of three segments—upper body, lower body, and helmet—which are joined together by airtight rings. The gloves are connected to the bottom of the sleeves by another set of rings. The outer shell of the suit is made from aluminum, and flexible joints at key points—shoulders and elbows, for example—allow for relative ease of motion. Beneath the shell is a polyurethane pressure bladder that is inflated to maintain adequate pressure on the body equivalent to that exerted by the atmosphere at the surface of Earth.

Inside this layer, astronauts wear a one-piece cooling and ventilation garment made

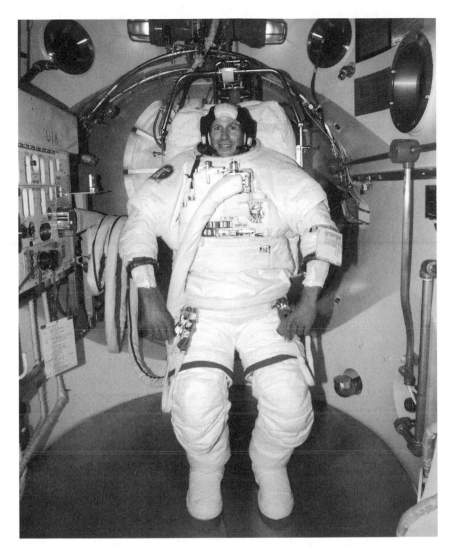

The shuttle space suit weighs 275 pounds and costs $1 million.

from spandex, which contains tubing through which water flows to maintain body temperature. Air ducts woven into the fabric of this garment allow air to circulate around the spacewalker's body. The water and air are stored in a life-support backpack attached to the outer shell of the suit. On the chest, a microcomputer lets the astronaut control the operation of the suit and, through a series of displays, allows him or her to monitor life-support functions and take corrective action before a problem becomes life threatening.

A Manned Maneuvering Unit (MMU) is also available, although it has not often been used on space walks since 1990. It's essentially a jet pack that propels the astronaut from place to place. Most of the work that space-walkers now do is such that they can move themselves around with the assistance of the shuttle robotic arm and handgrips in the cargo bay. Throughout their extravehicular activities, they remain tied to the shuttle by a retractable tether, removing the risk that they might drift off and be lost in space. Each shuttle carries two EMUs into space, and at least two astronauts on every mission are thoroughly trained in their use. Even when no extravehicular activity is planned, there is always the possibility that one might be required to make emergency repairs. For reasons of safety, two astronauts go on each EVA.

Suiting Up

The EMUs generate less pressure than exists inside the shuttle, 4.3 pounds per square inch as opposed to 14.2 pounds per square inch. Although the smaller pressure is adequate to sustain life, the astronauts must condition themselves to it gradually or they will get the bends, an often-fatal condition where nitrogen bubbles form in the blood and destroy organ tissue, including that of the brain. Therefore, twenty-four hours before an EVA is scheduled, the spacewalkers breathe pure oxygen for one hour to begin the process of removing nitrogen from their bodies. Then the pressure inside the orbiter is decreased to 10.2 pounds per square inch, and the amount of oxygen in the air supply is increased.

This acclimatization process continues after the astronauts put on their EMUs. Before leaving the air lock and emerging into space, they breathe pure oxygen for forty minutes while the pressure in their suits slowly drops to 5.3 pounds per square inch. Once they exit the air lock, the pressure continues to drop until it reaches its minimum of 4.3 pounds per square inch.

Earlier space suits required thirty minutes to put on, and the astronaut needed help from one of his or her crewmates. The EMU can be donned in five minutes by the wearer alone. Still, spacewalkers admit that they appreciate some help when getting ready for an EVA. First, they put on urine collection de-

How Astronauts Scratch Their Noses During Space Walks

NASA's engineers think of just about everything. The helmet of the extravehicular mobility unit (the space suit astronauts wear during space walks outside the shuttle) is equipped with a small V-shaped device just below the visor. By ducking their heads slightly, the astronauts can scratch itchy noses on it.

Its primary function, however, is to pinch the nostrils shut so the space walkers, by blowing air outward, can relieve pressure on their eardrums (make their ears pop) caused by the reduced air pressure inside their suits. The phenomenon is identical to that experienced by airline passengers when the cabin pressure drops.

vices similar to those used on liftoff. Then they open the door to the air lock, a five-foot-by-six-foot-nine-inch chamber where the space suits are stored. They put on the lower parts of their suits and then float into the upper parts, which are hanging on the wall. A third crew member helps them close the rings that lock the two parts of the suits together.

Next they pull on a tight-fitting cap—they call it a Snoopy cap—that contains all the equipment they'll need to communicate with the shuttle and mission control on the ground. Then their helmets are snapped into place and locked to the collars of the suits. Finally, the gloves go on. At this point the astronaut who has been helping the spacewalkers returns to the orbiter from the air lock and closes the hatch that separates the two. When the depressurization process is complete, the outer hatch of the air lock opens and the astronauts float out into the cargo bay.

Safety First

The first thing that the spacewalkers do after leaving the shuttle is attach their tethers, thin but strong wires, to a cable that runs the sixty-foot length of the cargo bay. They also attach a device called a manipulator foot restraint to the end of the robotic arm. This will enable them to lock their boots to the arm to give themselves a stable platform from which to work. One of the astronauts inside the shuttle can also move them safely from position to position by manipulating the arm.

In place of the bulky MMUs that early spacewalkers used, shuttle astronauts wear a less cumbersome jet pack called a Simplified Aid for EVA Rescue (SAFER). Should an astronaut accidentally become disconnected from a tether or foot restraint, the SAFER's small thruster engines will permit him or her to maneuver back to the shuttle. The SAFER attaches to the bottom surface of the space suit's backpack, and the astronaut can operate it from control panels on each side. For added safety, the SAFER will automatically right itself if the spacewalker starts to tumble.

There is little chance that a spacewalking astronaut will be swept away from the shuttle, even though they are both moving so quickly. The atmosphere around the vessel is too thin to exert a wind force, or drag, on an object with as small a surface area as the space suit. What little drag there is will be felt equally by the astronaut and the shuttle, and the absence of difference means they will stay in the same relative position to each other. If the improbable were to happen and an astronaut floated away, the shuttle could maneuver over and effect a rescue, but only if were is not docked to another space vehicle at the time.

Working on an EVA

Working outside the shuttle requires a great deal of strength and stamina. "The suit is bulky and stiff, which makes it difficult to bend or turn your body," says Pogue, who

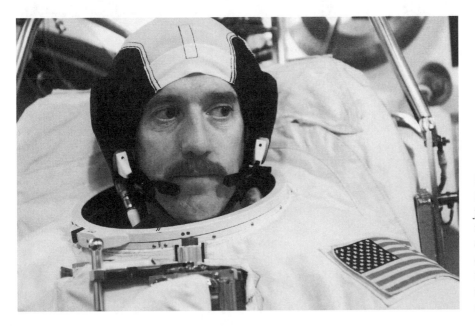

Space walkers wear Snoopy caps, tight-fitting headgear that contains equipment used to communicate with the shuttle and mission control on the ground.

performed two space walks, of six and a half and seven hours each, in an early version of the shuttle space suit.

The gloves are thick, so you don't have much feel. Because the air pressure in the gloves tends to hold the fingers out straight, it is very tiring to maintain a grip on anything. I always felt like a "bull in a china closet" when working in a space suit. After doing a lot of work in a suit, my finger tips became very sore and tender and I had cuts and burns on my shoulders from the braided metal arm-support cables inside the suit.[64]

Several minor improvements have made the EMUs somewhat more mobile since Pogue's space walks, but the gloves remain cumbersome. Moving hands and fingers still takes a lot of muscular effort, and hand and arm fatigue are common complaints among spacewalkers. The shuttle astronauts reported that their hands got too cold when they had to work for long periods out of the sunlight. For that reason, the glove was modified and the most recent version includes a heating element that keeps hands warm enough for the meticulous work the astronauts are required to do.

The shuttle orbits Earth every ninety minutes, and that means spacewalking astronauts have to do a lot of their work in darkness. Their helmets are equipped with lights to make this easier and safer. Working in the glare of the sun is also difficult. The visor of the spacewalker's helmet is coated with a gold

Since space walks can last for seven hours, an energy bar and a water bag with a straw are attached to space suits just below the neck.

oxide to reduce this effect, but it only works to a limited degree. It's a trade-off between reducing glare and allowing enough light through for the astronauts to see at all.

Since space walks can last for seven hours, the astronauts get hungry and thirsty. These needs, especially the need for water, have to be met or the spacewalkers might become so fatigued that they might not be able to complete their assignment. An energy bar and a water bag with a straw are attached by Velcro to the suit just below neck level. By ducking their heads downward, the astronauts can access each. It's not much for workers engaged in such strenuous activity, they complain, but it is enough to keep them going.

Saving the Hubble Telescope

The most challenging series of space walks ever undertaken were those to repair the Hubble Telescope, the world's first space telescope, which cost more than $10 billion to build and put into orbit. NASA justified the cost by claiming that the images the telescope transmitted of the farthest galaxies would revolutionize the study of astronomy. But after the Hubble was launched during a shuttle mission in 1990, the space agency discovered to its horror that the telescope's principal optical instrument was flawed, rendering the pictures it sent to Earth out of focus and almost useless. The public outcry at the waste of taxpayer dollars was so tumultuous, it threatened the future of the entire space program.

NASA resolved to attempt to repair the Hubble in the most daring shuttle mission up to that time. Engineers determined that the work would require five separate space walks, and NASA put together a crack team of astronauts under the direction of Story Musgrave, a space veteran who had made the shuttle's

Taking Time to See the Sights

Although astronauts are extremely busy during EVAs, they always try to take advantage of their unique perspective on the universe. In an interview with Karen Miller of NASA, Jim Reilly, who walked in space during a shuttle flight to the International Space Station in 2000, recalls a tip from Russian cosmonaut Yury Usachev, the commander of the space station at that time. After discussing the dangers that every EVA entails, Usachev said: "In spite of all that, when you're working, just make sure you take a couple of seconds to just look up every once in a while, and look around."

Reilly adds: "That was the best piece of advice he ever gave me. Every once in a while, just for 10 seconds, I'd stop and look around, and see what part of the planet I was over, and look at the horizon. . . . One time when I had a chance to hang out on the bottom of the space station, the sunset was coming. I left my lights off so I could watch the sun go down. And as it went down, the stars started popping out. Of course they don't twinkle."

first EVA in 1982. The training for the mission was intense, lasting for more than a year. Musgrave, then fifty-eight years old, and his crewmates committed thousands of separate procedures to memory and practiced them for thousands of hours in the water tank at the Johnson Space Center in Houston. By the time they had completed their training, Musgrave says, he could close his eyes and visualize every turn of every screw he would have to make during his space walks.

They were so well prepared for the mission that Musgrave insists he knew the exact position

Spacewalking is extremely difficult because the stiffness of space suits limits an astronaut's ability to move.

of every tool the repair team had at its disposal. "You could ask me halfway into [any of the space walks] where all three hundred tools were, and I could rattle them off,"[65] he says.

Musgrave likens spacewalking to ballet. "You have to worry about every finger and toe," he says. "If you've got a hand out of place in the ballet, you're going to lose style." But spacewalking is far more difficult than dancing because space suits severely limit an astronaut's range of motion. "Suits are hard," Musgrave says. "They're just miserable. Because

they're so stiff. . . . You learn a new body. You acquire a new arm. It's not your arm. The suit does not have the same joints you have, and you have to learn appropriately. If you think you're going to get into a suit and reach out for something, you're going to miss it."[66]

"The Most Demanding Job"

The space gloves were the most obstinate obstacle to overcome on the Hubble repair mission, Musgrave believes, comparing the hand fatigue he experienced fighting their rigidity to the experience of squeezing a tennis ball over and over again until the muscles in his hands and forearms ached and burned. He had to train himself to resist the natural urge to clasp objects. "Any time I see myself grabbing [during a space walk], I say, 'Is there another way to do it?' I don't grab things. I push and I touch."[67]

To install one component on the Hubble, Musgrave had to undo ten sets of connectors that were held in place by tiny screws, and he had to do this while hovering in space, his feet attached to the shuttle's fifty-foot robotic arm. "There were little connections at the back of this box, the size of what's in back of your PC [personal computer]," he recalls. "And they had little screws that were only about three millimeters long. I had a wrench that was three feet long. . . . That was the most demanding job I had ever done. I was on the edge of my ability."[68]

The complexity and difficulty of the job were compounded by weightlessness: every time Musgrave released one of the screws, it floated away and had to be retrieved. And, of course, this microgravity ballet was being conducted on an extremely delicate instrument, as Musgrave explains:

If you mistakenly touch the [Hubble's light-capturing] mirror, what you left would be on every single image that comes

The repair of the Hubble telescope (pictured) was a demanding mission. Spacewalkers had to perform complex tasks while hovering in space.

Space Walk Choreography

Veteran astronaut and spacewalker Story Musgrave described a shuttle extravehicular activity (EVA) as being a ballet. The metaphor is apt because inside the shuttle is a choreographer who supervises every move the spacewalkers make. On a 1999 mission to the International Space Station that role—its official designation is intravehicular (IV) crew member—was filled by Canadian astronaut Julie Payette. In this official NASA interview, she talks about her duties:

"During the EVA itself, I'll be sitting at the aft window of the space shuttle [using] the shuttle bay cameras . . . to see our crewmembers while they're doing their task outside. . . . I'll be the one talking to them, I'll be the one reminding them of some of the settings and some of the locations they have to go through and then answering any of the questions they might have about the details. So I'm the main communication between the crewmembers, the orbiter, and also to the ground. I'm basically supervising and monitoring the space walk. And when the crewmembers are ready to come back in, I'll be sure that they don't leave anything that we don't want to leave outside. We'll clean up the work site, come back into the hatch, and I'm the one that will help them repressurize the hatch and de-suit them after this long work."

Built into the EVA helmet's visor is a small television camera and two high-intensity lights. When a spacewalker is working outside the shuttle, both his or her crewmates inside the vessel and mission control officers and engineers back at the Johnson Space Center in Houston can see on their TV screens exactly what the astronaut on an EVA is looking at. This provides more than dramatic pictures. It enables the space walkers' support to help them solve technical problems at every step of the assignment.

down forever from the most powerful camera on Earth. A detail only the imagination could take care of is the workstation on your chest carrying all your tools, books, and tethers. In the clean room or water tank [during training] all that stuff hangs straight down. In zero G it'll hang straight out and get on the mirror.[69]

The mission was deemed a success, and when Musgrave and his crewmates returned to Earth, they were greeted with cheers from NASA brass and the public at large. But Musgrave knew that until the first full test was run and the Hubble started to transmit crystal-clear images, there was still a question mark hovering over all the hard work he and the other spacewalkers had done. "I put on a smile for people," he says. "But I felt humble and quiet." He was at home in Houston when the Hubble sent back a pristine picture of a distant galaxy called M-100. Only when he saw it with his own eyes did he breathe a sigh of relief. "My God," he recalls saying. "It's just gorgeous. . . . It's repaired!"[70]

Spacewalking became a crucial part of the shuttle missions devoted to the construction of the International Space Station. What the astronauts learned during the complicated repair of the Hubble Space Telescope has proved to be invaluable in the equally challenging work their EVA successors are performing on the space station and the even more daunting challenge future spacewalkers will have when they are faced with the task of building a human habitat on the surface of Mars.

CHAPTER 7

Exercise, Relaxation, and Rest

Working on the shuttle is both tiring and stressful, so NASA insists that the astronauts get adequate sleep and recreation. Like work, this aspect of life on the shuttle is carefully planned and operates on a timetable. Also, since muscles—including the heart—tend to atrophy after even a short period in weightlessness, daily exercise is prescribed. Both rest and exercise in microgravity present unique problems, and the astronauts have been inventive in overcoming them. Even something as elemental as sleep is not as easy in space as it is on Earth.

The Importance of Exercise

Most people accept that exercise is an important part of healthy living on Earth; that is even more true in space, where weightlessness deprives astronauts of muscle-toning activities, like lifting heavy objects and walking, available to their Earth-bound counterparts. The effects of microgravity on the body's most important muscle, the heart, are similar to those experienced by patients or invalids who are forced to spend a lot of time in bed. Cardiac deterioration begins after just a few days. Similarly, other muscles, freed from the stress of daily living in gravity, quickly start to shrink and weaken. Even on spaceflights of short duration, like most shuttle missions, the effects make themselves felt almost as soon as the gravitational force is removed.

An astronaut does his daily exercise to prevent muscle atrophy, a problem brought on by weightlessness.

NASA recommends one hour a day of some type of exercise for shuttle astronauts, and it is the duty of the mission commander to encourage them to do it. Many of them, like the majority of people on Earth, will

Many of the shuttle astronauts keep journals or diaries during their spare moments. They also take photographs to create a pictorial record of their adventure in space. The following passages are from a journal kept by Dr. Roberta Bondar during her mission in 1992. The entire journal is available on the Internet at www.seds.ca.

"Day Five: During the past days in space, the work has been carried on for 24 hours a day. The crew members . . . were divided into 'red' and 'blue' teams on 24-hour shifts. I was lucky enough to be on the blue (day) shift so that I could rest at night. We've been doing a lot of hard work, but we've also had time for fun and games. I played a starring role in The Great Coin Toss. During a live television broadcast today, me, clutching a coin in my hand, was flipped by two of my crew mates. . . .

Day Six: I saw my hometown, Sault Ste. Marie [in the Canadian province of Ontario] today as we quickly zipped passed it. . . . We couldn't see Canada and the entire earth at once. We saw different parts of it because the space shuttle wasn't far enough to see Earth as one big blue and white marble. To me, it looked like part of a large spinning ball."

avoid working out if they can get away with it. Mike Mullane admits he's been guilty of trying to shirk his exercise duties:

For missions less than 13 days in duration (most shuttle flights), flight surgeons require that exercise periods be scheduled. But whether the crew actually does exercise is optional. For missions longer than 13 days, the doctors require periodic exercise to keep the body's cardiovascular [heart and circulation] system conditioned and to minimize the potential for fainting on reentry and landing. When exercise is optional, there are two reasons many astronauts (myself included) skip it. First, an hour of exercise is an hour of window time that is lost. [Gazing at Earth through the shuttle's windows is a once-in-a-lifetime opportunity, and most astronauts want to take full advantage of it.] Second, getting hot and sweaty when there's no shower to step into doesn't make a lot of sense.[71]

William Pogue, who worked out on a stationary bicycle, explains that sweat, like all liquids, behaves differently in space from how it does on Earth—and the consequences are much more unpleasant. "Sweat [doesn't] drop off like it does here on Earth," he says.

The sweat on the back collected in a large puddle. By the end of half an hour of exercise, the puddle was as large as a dinner plate and about a quarter of an inch deep. It sort of slithered around on our backs. . . . When we were done, we had to move very carefully to avoid slinging off a large glob of sweat. It could have stuck to the walls of the spacecraft or onto equipment, and caused problems. We used an old towel to mop the sweat off our backs before bathing.[72]

Exercise Equipment

Nevertheless, NASA persists in sending a variety of workout equipment into orbit on the shuttle. That they devote storage space—a prized commodity in the orbiter—to it shows how important the flight doctors believe exercise to be for the well-being of the astronauts.

Luckily for payload managers, who calculate the cargo on each shuttle mission literally down to the ounce, free weights are useless in space. In the absence of gravity, a two-pound dumbbell and a 300-pound barbell weigh exactly the same—nothing. For resistance exercises, NASA provides bungee cords that the astronauts are encouraged to pull and twist to keep their muscles toned. For aerobic exercise, treadmills and stationary bicycles are available, although to conserve space only one or the other, not both, is supplied for a given mission.

Even here, microgravity has to be dealt with. Without some sort of restraint, an astronaut would simply float away from the equipment. Once again, bungee cords come to the rescue. Crew members fashion them into a harness to keep their feet in contact with the exercise equipment. Pogue, however, came up with another solution when he encountered the problem on a bicycle. "We finally took the seat off and held our heads against a makeshift pad mounted to the ceiling to balance the up-force caused by pushing against the pedals,"[73] he says.

There is one type of exercise that's not available on Earth, and it's also one that the astronauts enjoy. They call it astrobatics, and when practicing it, they take advantage of weightlessness to execute complicated acrobatic twists and turns while floating through the air. Astrobatics has therapeutic, as well as

To run on a treadmill, an astronaut must use a harness to keep her feet in contact with the equipment.

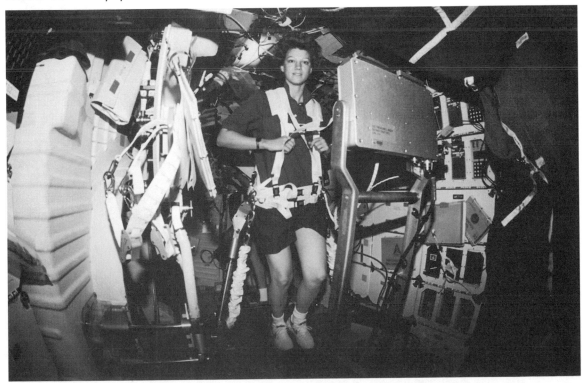

conditioning, value. "It's a good form of exercise not only for the body but for the mind," says space journalist Harry Stine. "It helps develop better kinesthetic abilities (knowing where the arms and legs are) as well as helping exercise the [balance mechanism of] the inner ear."[74]

The Importance of Doing Nothing

Like all people who work hard, shuttle astronauts look forward to rest and relaxation. The planners of early space missions devoted no thought to the importance of relaxation: the flights were short, the astronauts had too much

to do to allow for even brief periods of nonproductive activity, and they were recruited from the ranks of military test pilots, all of whom spend years being conditioned to function at a high level of efficiency in stressful situations where rest periods are not a realistic option. But as spaceflight became more routine and the corps of astronauts came to include men and women from nonmilitary backgrounds, recreation emerged as a subject for serious study by NASA doctors and psychologists.

"People cannot continue to operate efficiently or effectively without rest and recreation although they're given time away from their jobs to eat, sleep, and take care of bodily needs," says Stine, based on interviews with a number of astronauts and NASA offi-

A mission specialist relaxes by playing the saxophone.

cials. "Astronaut Gerald P. Carr reported, 'A guy needs some quiet time just to unwind if we're going to keep him healthy and alert up here. There are just two tonics to our morale—having time to look out the window and the attitude you guys (mission control) take and your cheery words.'"[75]

On the shuttle the day is divided into thirds: eight hours of work, eight hours of recreation, and eight hours of sleep. Flight planners strive to adhere to this schedule. In exceptional circumstances, they'll deviate to a twelve-four-eight plan, but they make every effort to get the crew back on the preferred routine as soon as possible. And although the rest periods are dictated, what the individual astronauts do on their free time is left entirely up to them.

Since many normal Earth pastimes are excluded—astronauts can't go bowling, fishing, or shopping while they're confined to the shuttle's crew quarters—most of them resort to reading, listening to tapes or compact discs through earphones, or watching DVD movies on their laptop computers. Some keep journals of their experiences, some call home (the astronauts are permitted a limited number of personal phone calls and e-mails that are transmitted through NASA's complicated communications network), and some just chat with their crewmates, who after months of training together are now also their friends.

Games Astronauts Play

To pass their free time, astronauts have taken advantage of their microgravity environment to invent games that are not possible on Earth. Peanuts and M&M's replace baseballs, basketballs, and footballs as toys. "Controlling a bouncing ball in weightlessness is tough," says William Pogue. "We had three small balls in the recreation kit, and we played with them

Space Poetry

Story Musgrave, a veteran of six shuttle flights, has found that contemplating space during his rest periods inspires him to write poetry. For example, these stanzas are excerpted from a poem called "Pockets Filled with a Picnic Lunch":

"My pockets filled with a picnic lunch,
I float into view of the spacecraft's windows;
they are filled with earth, heavenly earth.
She beckons and I follow . . .
. . . All too soon, this serene silent fall through the night
has moved the sun to the eastern horizon;
sunrise, another day, another journey, begin.
The earth beckons and I follow."

occasionally. When we threw them around, they bounced all over the place because of weightlessness. The hardest part was trying to find the ball when you were done. It's sort of like playing three-dimensional billiards."[76]

But nuts and candy keep the space travelers amused for hours. A crewmate taught Bill Nelson the M&M game.

Opening the package [of M&M's], he pulled one out and left it floating in midair in front of his face. Then, by gently blowing against it, he set it in motion across the cabin. By pushing off quickly, he could sail across the cabin, pass the M&M in flight, turn, and catch it in his mouth as it approached. Another trick was to release water in a big globule and then break it into little globules and catch them in one's mouth.[77]

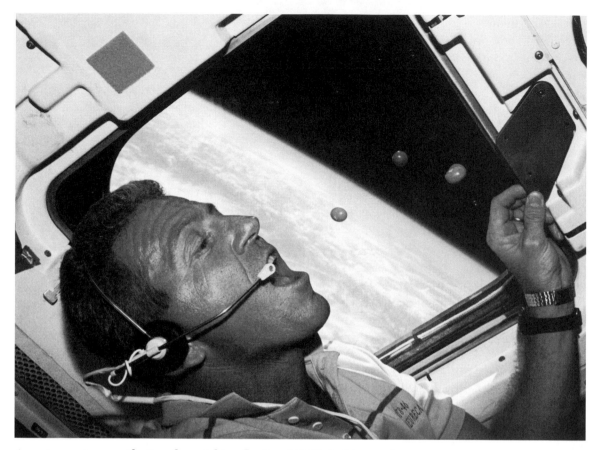

An astronaut passes the time by catching floating M&Ms in his mouth.

Flying paper airplanes is another popular pastime. With no gravity to pull them down, they sail through the air endlessly. But by far the favorite activity for all the astronauts is just gazing down at their home planet from their unique vantage point. "The sparkling blue oceans and bright orange deserts are glorious against the blackness of space," says Sally Ride.

Even if we can't see the whole planet, we can see quite a distance. When we are over Los Angeles we can see as far as Oregon; when we are over Florida we can see New York. We see mountain ranges reaching up to us and canyons falling away. We see huge dust storms blowing over deserts in Africa and smoke spewing from the craters of active volcanoes in Hawaii. We see enormous chunks of ice floating in the Antarctic Ocean and electrical storms raging over the Atlantic. . . . Since we see one sunrise and one sunset each time we go around the Earth, we can watch sixteen sunrises and sixteen sunsets every twenty-four hours.[78]

The view from space impressed on Bill Nelson how artificial the political barriers are that separate one people from another:

Looking at Earth from space was so much like looking at the big globe in my office that I found myself searching for the lines that divided Georgia from Florida, California from Nevada, and Mozambique from Malawi. There were no dividing lines, however. Seen from the perspective of space, political, racial, linguistic, and religious divisions all disappear. Looking at Earth from high up, I saw only one globe—a planet that is itself a fragile spaceship in the black void of space.[79]

Sleeping on Air

Adequate sleep is important to ensure that the astronauts remain alert and function at peak efficiency. Even minor slipups can have disastrous consequences in space. But sleep, like every other aspect of life on the space shuttle, presents the astronauts with a unique set of challenges. Some find it almost impossible to sleep soundly in weightlessness; others say microgravity is the most restful environment they've ever experienced. One thing is clear: space travelers need plenty of sleep to compensate for the unusual stress they are under during their waking hours. It is equally true that having sixteen sunrises and sunsets every twenty-four hours disrupts normal sleep patterns, but once again shuttle crews have brought a high degree of ingenuity to bear on the problem.

Most of the crew choose to use sleep restraints to keep them from being buffeted

The many contours of Earth's oceans, deserts, and forests present an awe-inspiring view against the blackness of space.

around the cabin by air currents generated by the ventilation system. These are cloth bags the astronauts can fasten to the walls or ceiling of the orbiter. They zip themselves inside, just like campers using sleeping bags, and the restraints both keep them warm and prevent them from floating into each other during sleep periods. Others forgo the restraints and opt to strap themselves into the permanent seats in the cockpit, even though bright sunlight streams through the windows when the shuttle is on the sunward side of Earth.

Story Musgrave usually shuns all restraints. "I have freefloated while sleeping and actually gone up into the flight deck, down into the mid-deck, and around," he says. "You bounce lightly off other sleeping people. Even if your face contacts the wall, it's so light you tend not to wake up." On his Hubble Telescope repair mission, Musgrave slept in the air lock with the four space suits taken on that flight. "They [the suits] looked like people with their own arms and legs," he recalls. "They'd grab onto me. As I'd float along, I could snuggle up inside the arms and rest there. I'd hug the suits and they'd hug me."[80]

All the astronauts are struck by one unusual phenomenon: when they're asleep their arms don't just hang by their sides. "The most bizarre thing about weightless sleep is that astronauts' arms float in front of their bodies when they're unconscious," Mullane says.

Sound asleep, an astronaut floats through the shuttle. Some astronauts prefer restraints while sleeping; others enjoy freefloating.

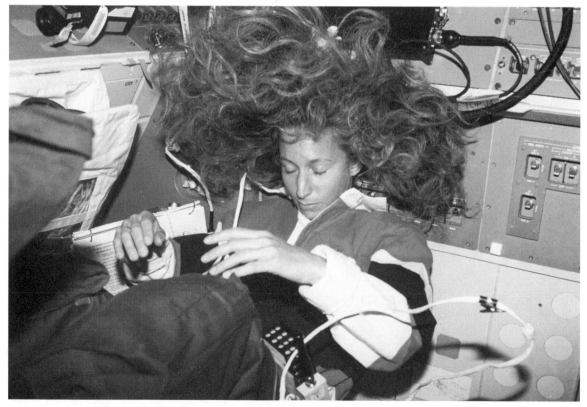

Three astronauts relax in their bunks aboard the space shuttle Endeavor.

Do Astronauts Snore in Space?

Snoring occurs when the glottis, a piece of fleshy tissue at the back of the throat, partially obstructs the flow of air in and out of the lungs. In the weightlessness of space, the force of gravity cannot hold the glottis in this position, so sustained snoring does not happen.

Astronaut Mike Mullane says he's never personally heard anyone snore in space, but adds that some of his colleagues have done so. In his book *Do Your Ears Pop in Space?* he points out: "One thing is certain about snoring in weightlessness. Rolling over isn't going to stop the noise. There's no such thing as rolling over in weightlessness. Every position is the same."

"The first time I awoke in the middle of a sleep period and saw my fellow crew members asleep on the wall with their arms gently waving in front of their bodies, I thought I was in a science fiction movie."[81]

Winding Down

Unless special circumstances require it, all shuttle astronauts sleep at the same time. The shuttle's computers and the crew at mission control monitor the craft performance. Should an emergency occur, an alarm would rouse the astronauts and they'd wake to the voice of a mission control engineer barking instructions to them through the ship's intercom.

Each sleep period is preceded by a winding-down time. It starts with a maintenance routine and ends with a moment of quiet reflection, as Bill Nelson explains:

Exercise, Relaxation, and Rest

After the last meal of each flight day, we would go into the presleep period, which was time for buttoning up the orbiter for the eight-hour interval. The crew configured all of the switches, established the proper attitude [position] for the spaceship in relation to the Earth, and got ready for bed. It was a good time for each of us to dwell in his own thoughts as we drifted off to sleep. . . . I think astronauts instinctively hold deep feelings inside—simply to survive in space. . . . My companions aboard the *Columbia* [the name of the orbiter Nelson flew on] were highly tuned, disciplined men who had little time to deal with emotions and feelings.[82]

Some astronauts resort to earplugs to block the constant humming of the shuttle's life-support systems, and others, like Sally Ride, use eye masks so they won't be disturbed by the endlessly rising sun. But, Ride says,

It's surprisingly easy to get comfortable and fall asleep in space. Every astronaut sleeps differently. Some sleep upside down, some sideways, some right side up. . . . I gather my bag, my sleep mask, and my tape player with earphones and float up to the flight deck. Then I crawl into the bag, zip it around me, and float in a sort of sitting position . . . right next to a window. Before I pull the mask down over my eyes, I relax for a while, listening to music and watching the Earth go by beneath me.[83]

While relaxation and sleep are important, most shuttle astronauts admit that the excitement of being in space makes it difficult for them to simply do nothing. Even rest periods in orbit are pulsating with excitement, and the space explorers can never shake off the feeling that they are living in perilous circumstances. As much as the shuttle comes to feel like a home away from home, they are aware that they are separated from a deadly environment only by a thin metal shell.

Coming Home

L
anding the shuttle tests the ability of its commander and pilot—and its on-board computers—severely. In just one hour, the orbiter is transformed from a space plane traveling at nearly eighteen thousand miles an hour into a quarter-million-pound glider that plummets through the atmosphere at such a high rate of speed that it glows like a red-hot coal. Because the shuttle has no jet engines, its maneuverability in the atmosphere is extremely limited. Also, once the decision to land has been made, there is no turning back. When atmospheric resistance begins to slow the vessel's speed below orbital velocity, nothing—and no one—can stop it from falling to Earth. For the astronauts, the shuttle's descent is every bit as nerve-racking as its liftoff.

Preparing and Packing

The de-orbit procedure takes eight hours and consists of undoing all the things the astronauts did after liftoff to prepare the shuttle for its mission. Communication antennas are retracted and the cargo bay doors are closed. If they fail to shut automatically, two members of the crew must don space suits and close them manually during an emergency space walk. The commander and pilot test the rocket thrusters to make sure they are all in working order. Exercise and other equipment is securely stowed away, temporary seats are retrieved from storage and bolted to the or-

biter's floor, and personal effects are put in lockers. The crew compartment is given a thorough cleaning—once the shuttle reenters the atmosphere, there will be no time to remedy even minor malfunctions caused by loose debris.

Then the astronauts have to find all the gear they wore during liftoff and put it on. Sometimes after an action-packed week or longer in space, they find it difficult to remember where they stowed things. Sally Ride admits she almost had to return to Earth barefoot when she couldn't find her boots at the completion of one of her flights. The astronauts don their pressure suits, which have pants that can be inflated to keep gravity from pulling blood away from their heads and into their legs, causing them to become light-headed or even black out.

For the same reason, four hours before landing, they drink thirty-two ounces of water to make sure they have adequate body fluids. They also take eight salt tablets to promote fluid retention. NASA doctors discovered in the early days of the space program that an astronaut loses, on average, 20 percent of his or her body fluids while in space. When they reenter the atmosphere and gravity causes blood to flow downward into the lower extremities, blackouts become a danger. The more fluids they have in their bodies, the more blood will remain in their brains, lessening the chance of this happening. Should the commander or pilot lose consciousness, the shuttle would run a high risk of crashing

Astronauts prepare to descend from space.

during the approach to the runway at the end of the flight.

In the midst of all the activity, the astronauts make sure to get one final look at Earth. For many, it will be the last chance they will ever have to observe their planet from the vantage point of space. Finally, and reluctantly, they strap themselves into their seats and wait for mission control to give them the final go-ahead to fire the engines that will start their journey home. Sometimes, as on liftoff, there are delays, usually caused by the weather. On Bill Nelson's flight, the crew had to go through the landing preparation proce-

dure three times before the weather cleared over their landing destination. "There was an immediate emotional and physical let-down," he says of the first delay. "Nevertheless, I had to admit that part of me was pleased to have another day in space: I had enjoyed it so much and was in no hurry for it to end."[84]

Gravity Returns

At L (landing) minus one hour and seventeen minutes, the commander receives the go/no go decision from mission control. Because the rockets that will fire to slow the orbiter are located in the aft fuselage, he must execute a maneuver that turns the vessel around so that it is flying backward. At L minus one hour and fifteen minutes, he presses a button on his control panel and the rockets ignite for two and a half minutes. This procedure reduces the craft's speed by about two hundred miles per hour. Even though the shuttle is still moving at approximately seventeen thousand miles per hour, the slight reduction in velocity is enough to lower the altitude of the orbit so that the vessel's trajectory intersects with the atmosphere, allowing friction to slow it down even more. To the astronauts, the firing of the engines registers only as a small jolt.

After the de-orbit burn is completed, the commander turns the orbiter around so that it is flying forward and adjusts the orientation of the nose to forty degrees above horizontal so that the craft will hit the atmosphere belly first. The shuttle's computerized guidance system keeps the craft within several tenths of a degree of its optimal inclination. Otherwise, Mike Mullane says, "if it flew too shallow of a reentry angle, it could skip on the air (like a flat stone can be made to skip on water) and fly far beyond its intended landing site. On the other hand, too steep a reentry angle [and] the shut-tle would dig into the thick part of the atmosphere and be torn apart by high G-loads."[85]

At forty minutes before touchdown, the commander dumps excess propellant from the reaction control engines, and five minutes later tells the crew to inflate their pressure suits. "We started to free-fall through space, gently pulled by Earth's gravity," Nelson says. "We descend from over one million feet above the Earth to 400,000 feet, traveling one-third of the distance around the world at the same time."[86]

At that point the atmosphere becomes thick enough for the astronauts to begin to feel the g forces it exerts. The shuttle is traveling at seventeen thousand miles per hour, and its rate of descent is increasing rapidly. "I could see the effects of gravity reappearing," Nelson says. "When I placed my tape recorder in front of me, it began to fall ever so slightly. . . . My helmet was starting to grow heavy. So were my feet. I had a feeling I was going to have a harder time readjusting to Earth's gravity than I had had adjusting to weightlessness."[87]

Blackout

The speed of the shuttle is so great as it crashes through the upper atmosphere that it

---

Landing Emergencies

Next to liftoff, landing the shuttle is the most dangerous part of a mission. The astronauts wear parachutes during both liftoff and descent, and if an emergency occurred while the vessel was on its way back to Earth, the following procedure would be followed: The astronauts would unstrap themselves from their seats and open the side hatch. They would then release a pole that is encased in a housing on the side of the orbiter, clip their parachute harnesses to the pole, and—one at a time—slide down it and under the wing. Once clear of the escape pole, they would open their parachutes and float to Earth. The procedure, which a crew of seven can carry out in about a minute, only works after the shuttle has descended to an altitude of approximately twenty-five thousand feet.

knocks electrons off the atoms that compose the molecules of the air. The resulting ions (atoms that have lost one or more electrons) and unattached electrons create an electrically charged envelope around the orbiter. This makes it impossible for the commander and mission control to communicate with each other. Also, ground computers and those on the shuttle can no longer exchange data. For the next thirteen minutes, until this blackout ends, the astronauts are on their own.

As friction on the fuselage of the orbiter increases, the vessel begins to heat and glow. "The blackness [of space] is replaced with the light show of air friction," says Mike Mullane.

> Nothing on the shuttle melts, but the air itself becomes so super-heated it glows. As the temperature increases, the glow changes from a red to an orange and finally to a pinkish color. . . . Air streams around the fuselage and wings and combines above the shuttle's upper windows. As it does so, its brightness intensifies. During a night-side reentry, this wake of hot air looks like flapping ribbons of fire. Flashes of it will shine through the two upper windows like flashes of lightning.[88]

By this time the force of gravity is sufficiently great that bits of debris that were overlooked during the pre-descent cleanup begin to rain down on the astronauts in their seats. Although the g forces experienced on landing are less than those of liftoff, at about two g's, they are enough to make the astronauts feel uncomfortable. Reports Mullane: "Because of the G-forces, a stomach-squeezing anti-G suit, and the fluid loading protocol, reentry feels as if you have a sack of cement on your shoulders, a belly button compressed to your back bone, a fluid-bloated stomach, and a distended bladder."[89]

Although the temperature of parts of the shuttle's hull reaches three thousand degrees Fahrenheit, the vessel's thermal protection tiles keep the internal temperature within normal ranges. In fact, the astronauts experience no sense that the craft is heating up at all. Also, up to this point, the descent has been free of the loud noise and violent shaking that accompanied blastoff.

From Spaceship to Glider

At L minus twenty minutes, the shuttle has slowed to fifteen thousand miles per hour. As it passes the 230,000-foot mark, the g forces reach their peak and the crew, for the first time, begins to feel the effects of their precipitous plunge through the atmosphere. "We begin to hear the rushing of wind, as we shoot through the thin air," says Sally Ride. "We feel a little vibration, like what passengers might feel on a slightly bumpy airplane ride. . . . We start to feel heavier and heavier. . . . It's an effort even to lift a hand."[90]

Bill Nelson adds:

> At 230,000 feet I felt turbulence. My recorder would no longer stay in the air. I could feel the blood draining out of my head and my helmet beginning to get loose as the puffiness in my face disappeared. I was also starting to become lightheaded, and my feet were hard to move off the floor. I turned the G-suit knob up to maximum pressure. . . . At Mach 18 [eighteen times the speed of sound], we were definitely feeling heavy. The atmosphere was tearing at the shuttle as we plunged back to Earth. . . . After having lived in space for six days, weighing zero pounds, the reintroduction to gravity was dramatic. I felt like I weighed two tons.[91]

The shuttle makes four S-shaped turns to reduce speed in preparation for landing.

At sixteen minutes before touchdown, the atmosphere has become thick enough for the shuttle's aerodynamic properties to come into play. By gently turning the craft's rotational hand control, a device in the cockpit that functions like a steering wheel, the commander manipulates the wing flaps to execute the first of four S-shaped turns. These sweeping maneuvers further slow the shuttle and bring it into alignment with the right glide path for landing.

"Now we were no longer a spaceship," Nelson says.

> We were a glider. It was up to our commander to fly and land just as he was trained. Hoot [Commander Robert "Hoot" Gibson] had practiced landing

over and over in the STA—the shuttle training aircraft. But if there was a miscue in practice, he always had an engine to fall back on. There was no such engine on the shuttle. To come in short now, or to overshoot the runway, would mean a hard landing in the desert mountains [near Edwards Air Force Base in California, the landing destination for Nelson's flight].[92]

Touchdown

At L minus six minutes, the shuttle is at ninety thousand feet and moving at 3.3 times the speed of sound. In spite of themselves, the astronauts think about how much has to go

Between Flights

After the shuttle lands at the Kennedy Space Center in Cape Canaveral, Florida, it is towed to the Orbiter Processing Facility (OPF) to be refurbished for its next flight. If weather conditions in Florida force it to land at one of the two alternative landing sites—Edwards Air Force Base in California or White Sands, New Mexico—it is first flown to Kennedy on the back of a modified 747 jetliner.

At the OPF a team of 160 technicians removes residual fuel from the orbital maneuvering system engines, inspects the heat-resistant tiles (and replaces any that are damaged), and removes the mission payload equipment. The orbiter's electronic and aviation systems are tested, and the ship is given a thorough cleaning. Then the next mission's payload is installed, and the main engines are checked to make sure they are working perfectly.

The orbiter is then moved to the Vehicle Assembly Building (VAB), where it is mated with a new liquid fuel tank and two refurbished solid rocket boosters. Once that is done, the assembled vessel is hoisted onto the back of a massive transport device called the Crawler and moved to the launchpad, where it is refueled. It remains on the launchpad for about a month before liftoff while a series of checks and rechecks is carried out.

---

right for their spaceship to land safely. "The question is, will there be a runway underneath it when it finally runs out of altitude?" says Mike Mullane. "It seems an impossible problem: over a 12,000-mile, 1-hour glide, it has to arrive at a 3-mile runway at the correct speed and altitude to land. And it has to do this without knowledge of many atmospheric variables that could severely affect the glide distance (e.g., upper atmospheric density and winds). How does it do it?"[93]

Three minutes before touchdown, the shuttle passes through the sound barrier. On the ground, spectators hear two loud sonic booms—one as the front end of the craft passes through the barrier and another as the aft end follows it. A minute later, at 13,300 feet altitude and a speed of 424 miles an hour, the commander takes over full control of the vehicle from the onboard computers. "*Columbia* was approaching nose down at an angle of 17 to 22 degrees," remembers Bill Nelson.

It looked and felt as if we were plunging straight for the Earth. . . . Hoot [Gibson] took manual control of the space plane. . . . He had to be careful not to lower his head for fear of getting dizzy. All the vital instruments in the cockpit were projected on his front windshield in what was known as a heads-up display. When [pilot] Charlie [Bolden], sitting in the right seat, said he had the runway in sight through the left window, Hoot refused to look, knowing that even the slightest tilt of his head could cause debilitating dizziness at what was an extremely crucial moment.[94]

At two thousand feet, traveling at 350 miles per hour, the commander executes a flare maneuver that causes the shuttle to abruptly pull up out of its steep dive. Ninety feet above the runway, the landing gear deploys. Fourteen seconds later, the shuttle's wheels touch the runway. "The landing gear slows us down, but we still land at about two hundred miles an hour—quite a bit faster than most airplanes," explains Sally Ride. "The rear wheels touch the runway first, so gently that inside we can't even be sure we've landed. Then the nose wheel comes down with a hard thump, and we know we're back on Earth."[95]

Good-bye to the Shuttle

The shuttle coasts to a stop along its 15,000-foot runway. Inside, the crew cheers the steely nerves and the expertise of the commander and pilot for bringing them home safely. But none of them bounds out of their seats. "I unstrap myself from my seat and try to stand up," Sally Ride recalls.

I am amazed at how heavy my whole body feels. My arms, my head, my neck—each part of me seems to be made of lead. It is hard to stand straight, it is hard to lift my legs to walk, and it is hard to carry my helmet and my books. I start down the ladder from the flight deck to the middeck—the same ladder that was unnecessary just an hour ago—and I have to concentrate just to place my feet on the

Shuttles land at approximately 200 miles an hour, much faster than most airplanes can land.

rungs. My muscles are nearly as strong as they were before the one-week space flight, but my brain expects everything to be light and easy to lift. My heart, too, has gotten used to weightlessness. For several days, it has not had to pump blood up from my legs against gravity. Now it is working harder again, and for several minutes after we land it beats much faster than normal. My sense of balance also

A crew poses in front of their space shuttle after landing safely at an air force base.

Lasting Effects of Spaceflight

Short-duration flights, such as those the shuttle makes, do not appear to leave the astronauts with any lasting negative effects. Muscle tone lost in weightlessness returns within a few days, as does normal balance. Some space travelers report lingering after-effects—pain in their joints and lower back—which last for several weeks or even months.

The effects of long-term spaceflights are a matter of serious study at NASA, which hopes to send a crew of astronauts to Mars by the year 2020. To this end, it monitors the health of all its astronauts to see if any problems emerge. So far the agency's doctors have determined that astronauts seem to enjoy the same life spans and to be subject to the same diseases as people who have never been in space.

needs to adjust to gravity. For a few minutes I feel dizzy every time I move my head. I have trouble keeping my balance or walking in a straight line for about fifteen minutes after landing.[96]

While the astronauts are getting their land legs back, the ground crew is busy making sure the orbiter is not leaking any harmful gas left over from the reaction control engine fuel. The space travelers do deep knee bends—Bill Nelson climbed up and down the ladder joining the flight deck and the mid-deck—to get enough strength back in their legs so they can walk off the shuttle under their own power and project the "right stuff" image that is still so important to NASA. A doctor comes on board to make sure there are no medical problems. About thirty minutes after the shuttle has landed, the crew emerge to the glare of photographers' flashbulbs and TV lights.

They also pause to take one last look at the spaceship that has given them a once-in-a-lifetime experience. "Once my feet are on the ground, I look back and admire the space shuttle," says Ride. "I take a few moments to get used to being back on Earth and to say goodbye to the plane that took us to space and back."[97]

Notes

Introduction: The Problems of Life in Space and How the Shuttle Solves Them

1. R. Mike Mullane, *Do Your Ears Pop in Space?* New York: John Wiley & Sons, 1997, p. 114.

Chapter 1: Training a Shuttle Crew

2. Bill Nelson with Jamie Buckingham, *Mission: An American Congressman's Voyage into Space.* San Diego: Harcourt Brace Jovanovich, 1988, p. 40.
3. Mullane, *Do Your Ears Pop in Space?* p. 209.
4. G. Harry Stine, *Living in Space.* New York: M. Evans and Company, 1997, p. 130.
5. Henry S.F. Cooper Jr., *Before Lift-Off: The Making of a Space Shuttle Crew.* Baltimore: Johns Hopkins University Press, 1987, p. 106.
6. William R. Pogue, *How Do You Go to the Bathroom in Space?* New York: Tom Doherty Associates, 1999, pp. 152–53.
7. Nelson, *Mission*, pp. 64–65.
8. Mullane, *Do Your Ears Pop in Space?* p. 205.
9. Nelson, *Mission*, p. 62.

10. NASA, "Astronaut Training," in *Space Shuttle News Reference Manual.* Kennedy Space Center, Cape Canaveral, FL: National Aeronautics and Space Administration, undated, p. 3.
11. Quoted in Cooper, *Before Lift-Off*, p. x.
12. Cooper, *Before Lift-Off*, pp. 34–35.
13. Cooper, *Before Lift-Off*, p. 35.
14. Quoted in Cooper, *Before Lift-Off*, p. 33.
15. Mullane, *Do Your Ears Pop in Space?* p. 28.
16. Quoted in Cooper, *Before Lift-Off*, p. 200.

Chapter 2: Blastoff

17. Sally Ride with Susan Okie, *To Space and Back.* New York: Beechtree, 1986, p. 13.
18. Nelson, *Mission*, p. 16.
19. Quoted in Cooper, *Before Lift-Off*, p. 208.
20. Nelson, *Mission*, pp. 13–15.
21. Mullane, *Do Your Ears Pop in Space?* p. xi.
22. Mullane, *Do Your Ears Pop in Space?* p. xii.

23. Ride, *To Space and Back*, p. 17.

24. Nelson, *Mission*, p. 111.

25. Nelson, *Mission*, pp. 114–15.

26. Nelson, *Mission*, p. 115.

27. Nelson, *Mission*, p. 117.

28. Ride, *To Space and Back*, p. 18.

Chapter 3: Adapting to Microgravity

29. Pogue, *How Do You Go to the Bathroom in Space?* p. 26.

30. Nelson, *Mission*, p. 187.

31. Mullane, *Do Your Ears Pop in Space?* p. 71.

32. Pogue, *How Do You Go to the Bathroom in Space?* p. 98.

33. Pogue, *How Do You Go to the Bathroom in Space?* p. 26.

34. Mullane, *Do Your Ears Pop in Space?* p. 143.

35. Mullane, *Do Your Ears Pop in Space?* p. 144.

36. Pogue, *How Do You Go to the Bathroom in Space?* p. 78.

37. Pogue, *How Do You Go to the Bathroom in Space?* p. 23.

38. Mullane, *Do Your Ears Pop in Space?* p. 146.

39. Pogue, *How Do You Go to the Bathroom in Space?* pp. 32–33.

40. Ride, *To Space and Back*, pp. 29–32.

Chapter 4: Food and Hygiene

41. Nelson, *Mission*, p. 135.

42. Nelson, *Mission*, p. 47.

43. Nelson, *Mission*, p. 47.

44. Ride, *To Space and Back*, pp. 35–39.

45. Ride, *To Space and Back*, p. 42.

46. Nelson, *Mission*, p. 135.

47. Nelson, *Mission*, p. 136.

48. Ride, *To Space and Back*, p. 42.

49. Quoted in Stine, *Living in Space*, p. 122.

50. Mullane, *Do Your Ears Pop in Space?* p. 120.

51. Mullane, *Do Your Ears Pop in Space?* p. 120.

52. Ride, *To Space and Back*, p. 50.

53. Ride, *To Space and Back*, pp. 49–50.

Chapter 5: Working

54. Mullane, *Do Your Ears Pop in Space?* pp. 107–8.

55. Barbara Bondar and Dr. Roberta Bondar, *On the Shuttle: Eight Days in Space*. Toronto: Greey de Pencier Books, 1993, p. 46.

56. Ride, *To Space and Back*, p. 54.

57. Mullane, *Do Your Ears Pop in Space?* p. 30.

58. Ride, *To Space and Back*, pp. 58–59.

59. Nelson, *Mission*, p. 192.

60. Bondar and Bondar, *On the Shuttle*, pp. 24–25.

61. Bondar and Bondar, *On the Shuttle*, p. 26.

62. Bondar and Bondar, *On the Shuttle*, p. 30.

Chapter 6: Space Walks

63. Lillian D. Kozloski, *U.S. Space Gear: The Outfitting of an Astronaut*. Washington, DC: Smithsonian Institution Press, 1994, p. 125.

64. Pogue, *How Do You Go to the Bathroom in Space?* pp. 43–44.

65. Quoted in Andrew Chaikin, "Ballet in Space: How to Be a Hubble Space Walker," *Space and Science*, December 1999, p. 4.

66. Quoted in Chaikin, "Ballet in Space," pp. 2, 4.

67. Quoted in Chaikin, "Ballet in Space," p. 4.

68. Quoted in Chaikin, "Ballet in Space," p. 5.

69. Quoted in Nina L. Diamond, "Story Musgrave: Space Walk," *Omni*, August 1994, p. 9.

70. Quoted in Chaikin, "Ballet in Space," p. 5.

Chapter 7: Exercise, Relaxation, and Rest

71. Mullane, *Do Your Ears Pop in Space?* pp. 132–33.

72. Pogue, *How Do You Go to the Bathroom in Space?* p. 68.

73. Pogue, *How Do You Go to the Bathroom in Space?* p. 68.

74. Stine, *Living in Space*, p. 178.

75. Stine, *Living in Space*, p. 172.

76. Pogue, *How Do You Go to the Bathroom in Space?* p. 84.

77. Nelson, *Mission*, p. 129.

78. Ride, *To Space and Back*, pp. 21–25.

79. Nelson, *Mission*, p. 144.

80. Quoted in Diamond, "Story Musgrave," p. 7.

81. Mullane, *Do Your Ears Pop in Space?* p. 131.

82. Nelson, *Mission*, pp. 142–43.

83. Ride, *To Space and Back*, pp. 45–46.

Chapter 8: Coming Home

84. Nelson, *Mission*, p. 160.

85. Mullane, *Do Your Ears Pop in Space?* p. 150.

86. Nelson, *Mission*, p. 166.

87. Nelson, *Mission*, pp. 166–67.

88. Mullane, *Do Your Ears Pop in Space?* p. 157.

89. Mullane, *Do Your Ears Pop in Space?* p. 157.

90. Ride, *To Space and Back*, p. 81.

91. Nelson, *Mission*, p. 168.

92. Nelson, *Mission*, p. 168.

93. Mullane, *Do Your Ears Pop in Space?* pp. 152–53.

94. Nelson, *Mission*, p. 169.

95. Ride, *To Space and Back*, p. 86.

96. Ride, *To Space and Back*, p. 88.

97. Ride, *To Space and Back*, p. 90.

For Further Reading

Books

Don Berliner, *Living in Space*. Minneapolis: Lerner Publications, 1993. A brief, well-illustrated introduction to the problems of life in space and the solutions that NASA and the Russian space program have devised to surmount them.

Marianne J. Dyson, *Space Station Science: Life in Freefall*. New York: Scholastic, 1999. Provides scientific background to various aspects of living in space, including life on the shuttle, in a lively and easy-to-understand way. The book is illustrated with helpful drawings and includes experiments that can be done at home.

Kerry Mark Joels and Gregory P. Kennedy, *The Space Shuttle Operator's Manual*. New York: Ballantine Books, 1988. This book imaginatively puts the reader in the space shuttle commander's chair and takes him or her through a fairly detailed typical mission, from liftoff to touchdown. There's a lot of technical detail about the shuttle and its operations, but the material is presented in a way that makes it easy to grasp. However, the book does not include recent modifications made to the shuttle. Luckily, these alterations were minor and the vast majority of the information provided is current.

Gregory L. Vogt, *Spacewalks: The Ultimate Adventure in Orbit*. Berkeley Heights, NJ: Enslow Publishers, 2000. A simplified introduction to extravehicular activities, illustrated with photographs and anecdotes from a number of shuttle space walks.

Internet Resources

There is a wealth of information about life on the shuttle available on NASA's many websites. Unfortunately, these sites are not well integrated, not all of them have search engines, and those that do tend to return a large number of references that are only marginally relevant to the subject of the inquiry. NASA itself acknowledged the chaotic nature of its Internet presence when a spokesman told a reporter for the Associated Press early in 2001—in response to a question about a virus attack—that the agency did not, in fact, know how many websites it operated. The best way to access the information NASA has to offer—and there is a lot of it—is to type search words into a general web browser (Google, AltaVista, etc.) and follow the links that come up. For those who want to probe the NASA websites directly, the following URLs are good places to start: www.spaceflight.nasa.gov, www.hq.nasa.gov/osf, www.shuttle.nasa.gov, spacelink.nasa.gov

Works Consulted

Books

Barbara Bondar and Dr. Roberta Bondar, *On the Shuttle: Eight Days in Space*. Toronto: Greey de Pencier Books, 1993. Roberta Bondar, with the help of her writer sister, Barbara, relives her eight days on the shuttle as a science specialist in 1992. The text is illustrated with numerous full-color pictures and includes an informative account of the challenges and rewards of conducting scientific experiments in space.

Henry S.F. Cooper Jr., *Before Lift-Off: The Making of a Space Shuttle Crew*. Baltimore: Johns Hopkins University Press, 1987. A detailed description of how a shuttle crew trains for a mission, from induction into the astronaut corps to liftoff. Based on interviews and observations during the preparation for shuttle mission 41-G, which took place in October 1984.

Lillian D. Kozloski, *U.S. Space Gear: The Outfitting of an Astronaut*. Washington, DC: Smithsonian Institution Press, 1994. The author, a former staffer in the department of space history at the Smithsonian Institution's National Air and Space Museum, chronicles the history of space suits from the earliest manned spaceflights to the shuttle. Well illustrated and somewhat technical.

R. Mike Mullane, *Do Your Ears Pop in Space?* New York: John Wiley & Sons, 1997. In question-and-answer format, astronaut Mullane discusses his experiences on the space shuttle; easy to read, humorous, and illustrated with many personal anecdotes.

NASA, "Astronaut Training," in *Space Shuttle News Reference Manual*. Kennedy Space Center, Cape Canaveral, FL: National Aeronautics and Space Administration, undated. This lengthy document is updated regularly to provide members of the media with current information on the space shuttle and its operations. The material is highly technical and very thorough.

———, *NASA Facts*. Lyndon B. Johnson Space Center, Houston, TX: National Aeronautics and Space Administration, undated. A series of brief, nontechnical papers on various aspects of spaceflight, including the shuttle.

Bill Nelson with Jamie Buckingham, *Mission: An American Congressman's Voyage to Space*. San Diego: Harcourt Brace Jovanovich, 1988. Nelson, who was chairman of the House of Representatives' Space Science and Applications subcommittee at the time of his flight in 1986, provides a colorful account of life on the shuttle from the perspective of a nonprofessional astronaut. Along with coauthor Jamie Buckingham, he re-creates the experience of spaceflight in a candid and readable way.

William R. Pogue, *How Do You Go to the Bathroom in Space?* New York: Tom Doherty Associates, 1999. Veteran astronaut and spacewalker Pogue, who spent time on Skylab—the first U.S. space station—has updated his account of the problems of living and working in space to include information gleaned from his shuttle colleagues. The anecdotal material deals with all aspects of the astronaut experience and is presented in question-and-answer format.

Sally Ride with Susan Okie, *To Space and Back*. New York: Beechtree, 1986. Ride, America's first woman astronaut, along with coauthor Okie, describes living and working on the shuttle in a lively and anec-dotal way. The book contains many striking color photographs.

G. Harry Stine, *Living in Space*. New York: M. Evans and Company, 1997. A study of the physical and psychological implications of life beyond Earth's atmosphere, relevant to both short-duration flights like those of the space shuttle and longer-duration stays on space stations and vessels undertaking interplanetary voyages.

Periodicals

Nina L. Diamond, "Story Musgrave: Space Walk," *Omni*, August 1994. An interview with astronaut Story Musgrave about his experiences as a shuttle crew member and spacewalker. The focus is on his 1993 mission to repair the Hubble Space Telescope.

Andrew Chaikin, "Ballet in Space: How to Be a Hubble Space Walker," *Space and Science*, December 1999. The article discusses how Story Musgrave prepared for and carried out the difficult shuttle mission to repair the Hubble Space Telescope in 1993.

Internet Resources

liftoff.msfc.nasa.gov/news. This is the news site for NASA's Marshall

Space Flight Center in Huntsville, Alabama. It is a good source of up-to-date information on space exploration and astronomy. It also includes interviews with astronauts and other NASA personnel.

spacestory.com. This site is maintained by veteran astronaut and space-walker Story Musgrave. It includes examples of his space photography as well as biographical information and selections from his poetry, diaries, and interviews.

users.aol.com/kenjenks/personal. NASA computer expert Ken Jenks introduces himself and his passion for publishing science fiction on the World Wide Web.

Index

Picture Credits

Cover photo: © NASA

© Hulton/Archive by Getty Images, 24, 34, 80, 94

Chris Jouan, 11 (top)

NASA, 9, 11 (bottom), 13, 16, 17, 18, 19, 21, 22, 26, 27, 28 (left and right), 29, 32, 35, 37, 38, 39, 40, 42, 44, 50, 54, 56, 59, 62, 63, 64, 65, 69, 71, 72, 74, 75, 77, 79, 83, 91, 93

© NASA/CORBIS, 85

© NASA/Roger Ressmeyer/CORBIS, 48, 51, 53, 55, 82, 84, 88

About the Author

Robert Taylor has written on science, technology, history, politics, law, philosophy, medicine, and contemporary culture. He lives in West Palm Beach, Florida.